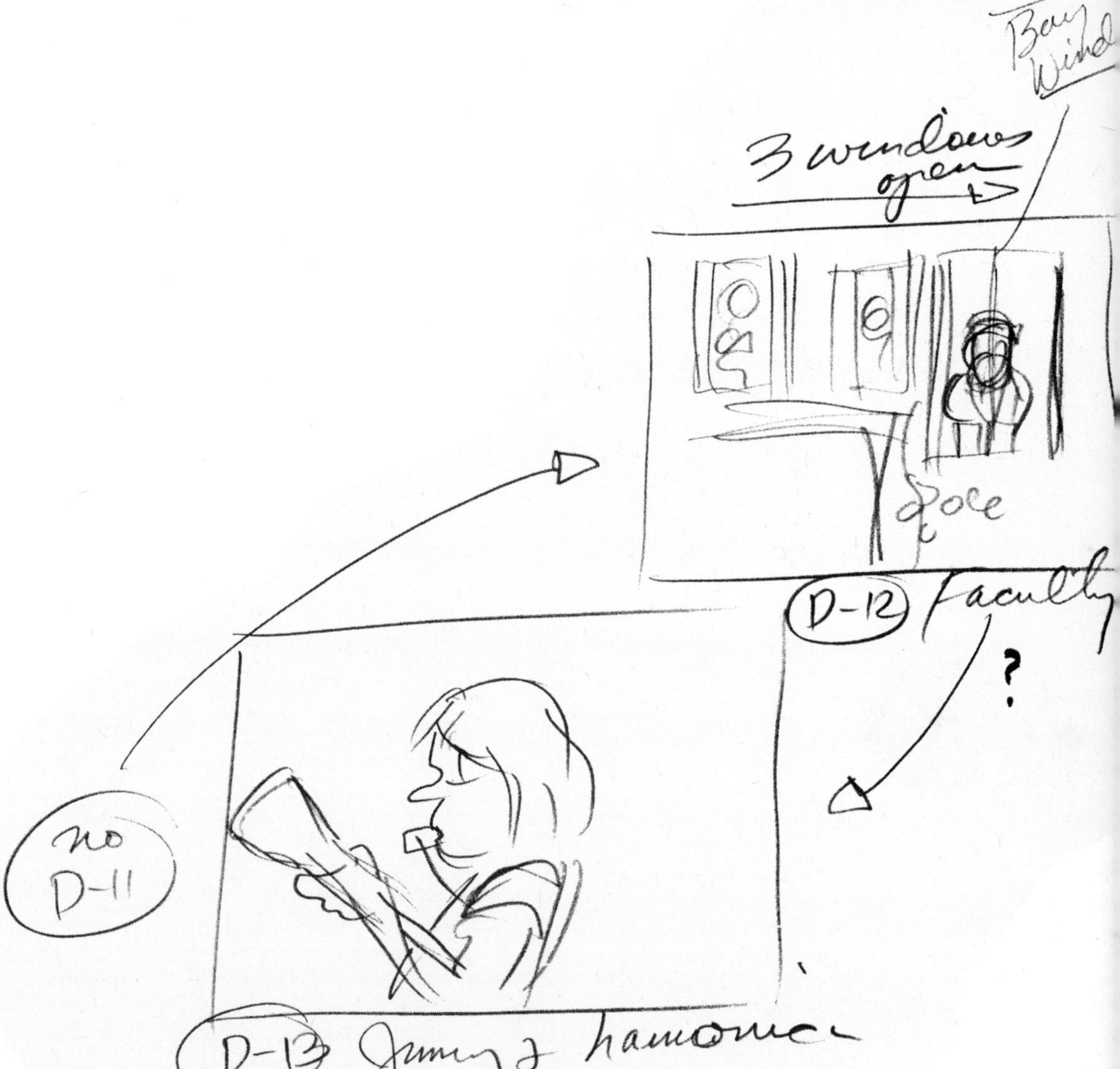
3 windows open
D-12 Faculty
?
no D-11
D-13 Jimmy & harmonica
OK

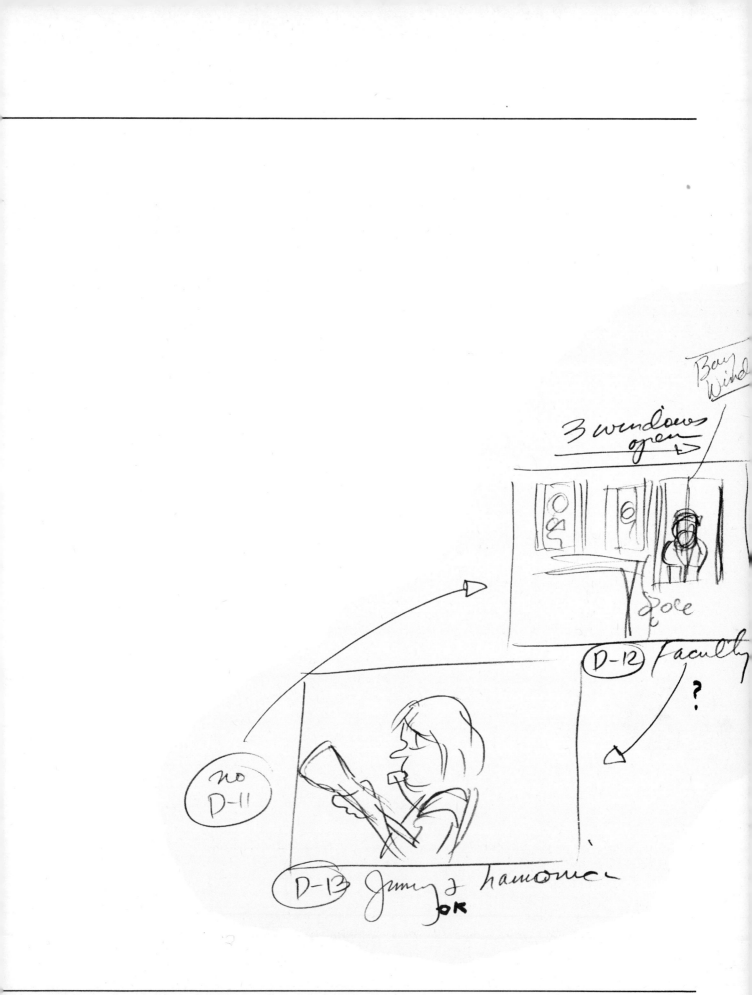

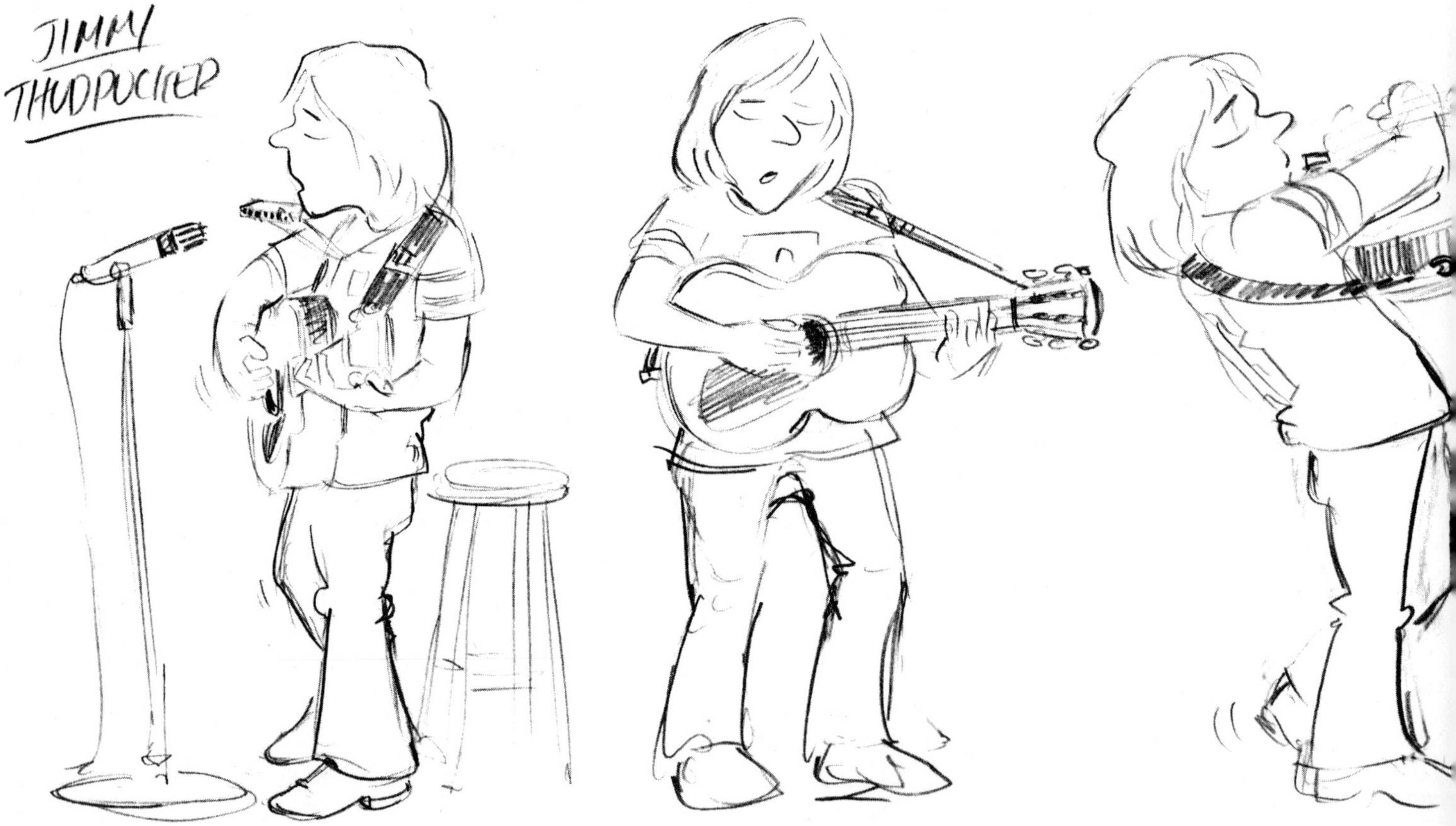
JIMMY THUDPUCKER

John & Faith Hubley's

A

GY 16
R.R 12
BR 19
OY 15
X-BC 3
BR 19

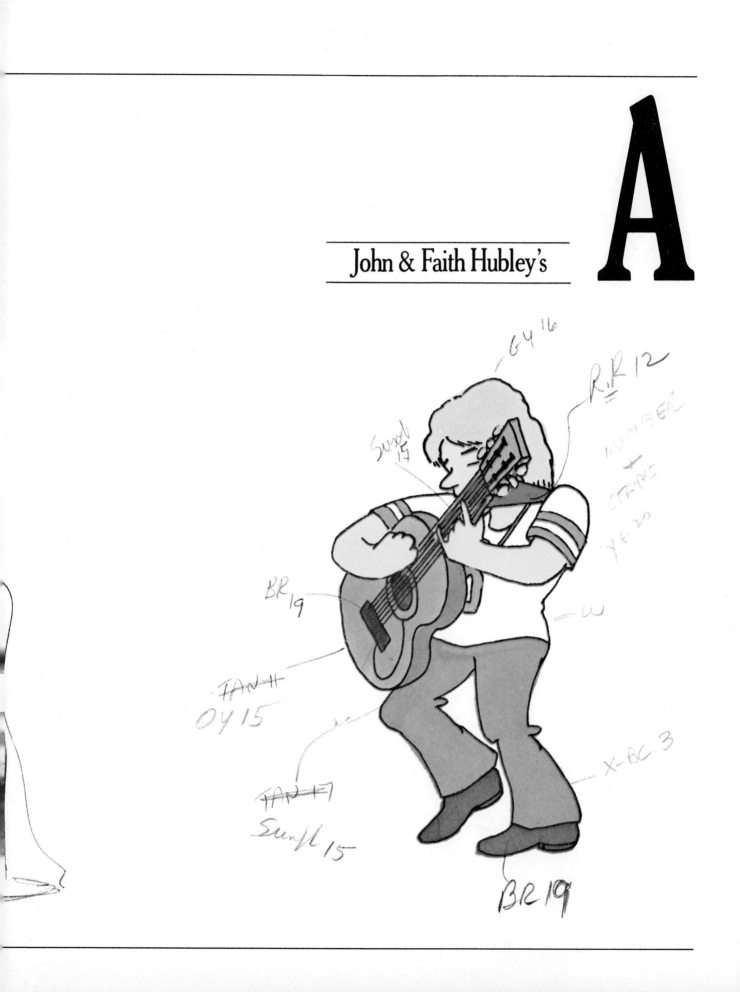

Doonesbury

Thudpucker Sings

I do believe, yes, I do believe
A day will come
When all mankind

Special

A Director's Notebook
by Garry Trudeau

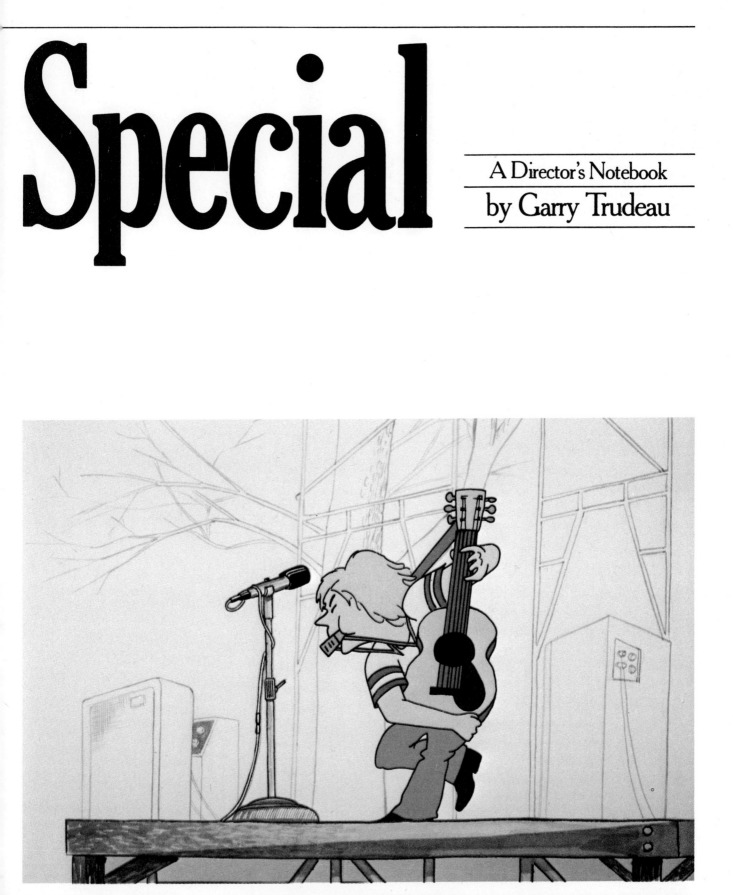

Sheed Andrews and McMeel, Inc. Subsidiary of Universal Press Syndicate **Kansas City**

Other Doonesbury Books

Still a Few Bugs in the System
The President Is a Lot Smarter Than You Think
But This War Had Such Promise
Call Me When You Find America
Guilty, Guilty, Guilty!
"What Do We Have for the Witnesses, Johnnie?"
Dare To Be Great, Ms. Caucus
Wouldn't a Gremlin Have Been More Sensible?
"Speaking of Inalienable Rights, Amy…"
You're Never Too Old for Nuts and Berries
An Especially Tricky People
As the Kid Goes for Broke
Stalking the Perfect Tan
The Doonesbury Chronicles

Introduction reprinted with permission from TV Guide Magazine.®
Copyright © 1977 by Triangle Publications, Inc., Radnor, Pennsylvania

A Doonesbury Special copyright © 1978 by Garry Trudeau.
Material from the NBC television special, "A Doonesbury Special," copyright © 1977
by John and Faith Hubley Films, Ltd.
Preface copyright © 1978 by Faith Hubley.
The animated film "A Doonesbury Special" is distributed by Pyramid Films.
All rights reserved. Printed in the United States of America. No part of this book may
be used or reproduced in any manner whatsoever without written permission except in
the case of reprints in the context of reviews. For information write Sheed Andrews
and McMeel, Inc., Subsidiary of Universal Press Syndicate, 6700 Squibb Road,
Mission, Kansas 66202.
Designer: Jean-Claude Suarès
Assistant Designer: Susan Willmarth
Production: Joe Teodorescu
Typesetting: Haber Typographers Inc., New York
Library of Congress Catalog Card Number: 77-95202.
ISBN: 0-8362-1104-9 hardbound
        0-8362-1103-0 paperback

W hen Garry Trudeau asked Johnny and me to produce *A Doonesbury Special,* we were thoroughly delighted. John had been one of Garry's teachers at Yale in the good old days of the early seventies, and they were equally impressed with the other's talents. I strongly agreed with both of them in this mutual assessment.

We began work with Garry in November of 1976. And as work progressed, Garry's "perfect pitch" (my shorthand for a highly developed intuition for sound and image) made collaboration with him a romp. The storyboard, and then the sound track, developed midst roars of laughter as we acted out all the parts and resolved our differences of opinion two against one. When the board and sound track were completed and approved, we began work on "thumbnails," a more refined breakdown of the script into specific scenes with directions for the animators.

Shortly thereafter, Johnny became gravely ill; and then, in February, he died. His absence left us in a state of shock and sorrow, and Garry and I deliberated long and hard over whether we could finish the film without him. Despite our fears and anxieties we decided to plow ahead; and everyone involved—animators, artists, camera people, techies, the lab and network—pulled together and excelled in their crafts.

This was Johnny's last film, and in many ways, a poignant exit.

Johnny was always interested in new forms. The process of breathing cinematic life into Garry's compelling collection of characters was a most rewarding challenge to us both. I am very gratified by the results of our endeavor and take real pleasure in this small volume.

PREFACE
by Faith Hubley

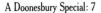

INTRODUCTION

by Garry Trudeau

When John Hubley died last February midway through the filming of *A Doonesbury Special*, the shock was felt throughout the world's animation community. He left behind him countless admirers and a body of work that had earned him and his wife Faith international critical acclaim and three Academy Awards. And yet among certain of his peers, Hubley will probably be best remembered as an outsider, a brash iconoclast who was among the first of his generation to challenge the long undisputed arbiter of animation technique, Walt Disney.

Not that he hadn't earned the right. Hubley had, in fact, toiled for many years in the Disney shop, first as a background artist on *Snow White*, and later as an art director on *Pinocchio* and "The Rite of Spring" segment of *Fantasia*. But by the late forties, Hubley and several other Disney artists (including Pogo creator Walt Kelly) had become disenchanted enough with the cloying and morally simplistic Disney to break away on their own. In 1955, Hubley started his own company, Storyboard, Inc., where, in partnership with his wife, he began to create the extraordinary films that were to prove such a radical departure from the traditions he himself had helped to establish. Gone were the coy bunny rabbits and pigs, the archetypical hero-princesses and queen-witches, the formal storytelling and the contrived dialogue. In their place, the Hubleys created an open-ended impressionistic universe in which characters assumed the painterly shapes best suggested by their personalities and spoke in dialogue that was alternately forceful, halting, exuberant, inaudible, spontaneous and overlapping—in short, the way people really

talk. And as Hubley's animating vocabulary changed, so, too, did his purposes. As the years went by, he became overwhelmed by the possibilities of his medium. "These aims seem realizable," he wrote, "to increase awareness, to warn, to humanize, to elevate vision, to suggest goals, to deepen our understanding of ourselves and our relationships with each other."

Preposterous aspirations for a medium so denigrated as animation, but it was within these notions that I as a comic strip writer first discovered a common purpose with the Hubleys. Since their invention some seventy-five years ago, comic strips have suffered from a comparable suspicion that cartoon images are somehow not respectable and certainly not to be taken seriously. While much of today's output would tend to validate this assumption, there is also the troublesome fact that almost *everyone* reads them. Over 90 percent of the people who pick up a newspaper read the comics; in fact, the only part of the newspaper that is more widely read is the front page. With a comic-page readership estimated at over 90 million, one might hope and even assume that a great deal would be happening on there, that the sheer vastness and heterogeneity of the audience would insure a forum accommodating a wide array of conceptual approaches, from the strictly entertaining to the utterly subversive. Of course, no such diversity exists, nor is it ever likely to as long as editors and artists continue to perceive comic strips as simple soap opera and low-rent vaudeville. Although there has been a handful of notable exceptions, most comic strip artists have intentionally aimed low. In the name of preserving family values, they have scrupulously avoided exploring the almost limit-

less possibilities the medium has for communicating ideas and provoking their audiences to thought and judgment.

It was in such a mind that I began writing in 1970, and it was three years later, as an art student, that I found a kindred spirit in one of my professors, John Hubley. To my delight and surprise, he and his wife were the first to suggest that *Doonesbury* might lend itself to animation. Hubley did not regard the unusually static quality of the drawings as a drawback, because he felt that in the presence of strong characterizations, certain dynamics would inevitably suggest themselves. He believed strongly that any aspect of the process of human growth could be symbolized and that no idea was too weighty to be dramatized visually.

While this sort of celebration of the inner self is hardly new to graduates of the Actors' Studio, it is something quite innovative for animation. While the Disney iconography did in fact include many marvelous characterizations, the animators generally drew their inspiration from meticulously observed stereotypes, from the beguiling Dopey to the chronically dour Grumpy. Moreover, Disney characters were static, their personalities locked in the demands of the roles they were assigned.

In vivid contrast, Hubley's characterizations were built around highly individualized, evolving human behavior. As a consequence, we spent long hours analyzing the idiosyncracies and motivations of my characters. And once the Hubleys felt they knew the *Doonesbury* people reasonably well, the process was repeated for the animators. Animators are in many respects like frustrated actors, and while working on a certain scene, they can agonize for days over whether a certain nuance or gesture is in charac-

ter. In my sessions with them, I was repeatedly called upon to articulate the essence of my characters, something I found unusually difficult to convey, since the decisions I had made in their creation were largely intuitive. What was at the root of Zonker's ingenuousness? Of Mark's need for continuity? Of B.D.'s obstinacy? I hadn't the faintest idea. While I cared deeply about all of them, my position had always been that once conceived, they were on their own.

Neither the animators nor the actors who were to play the voices found this attitude remotely helpful, but the characters finally jelled and somehow the film was brought to completion. Although John was not to survive the project, the momentum had been established before his death, and Faith Hubley ably finished the film we had set out to make. While some of what John must have envisioned was undoubtedly lost in the final product, *A Doonesbury Special* stands as fitting testimony to the sane and compassionate sensibilities of one of animation's first true visionaries.

A Doonesbury Special

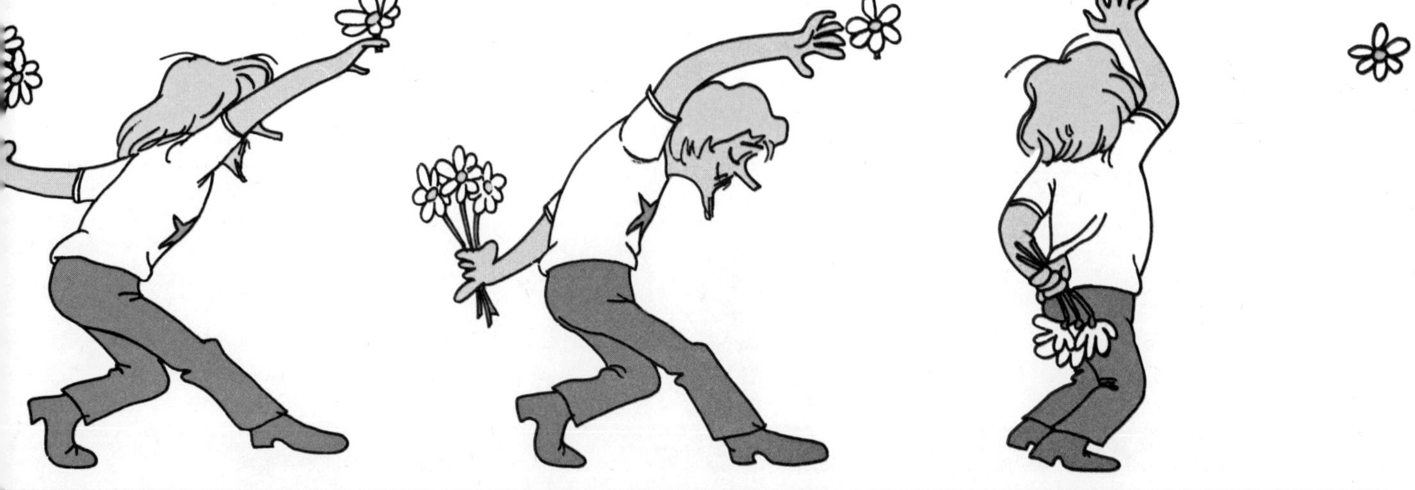

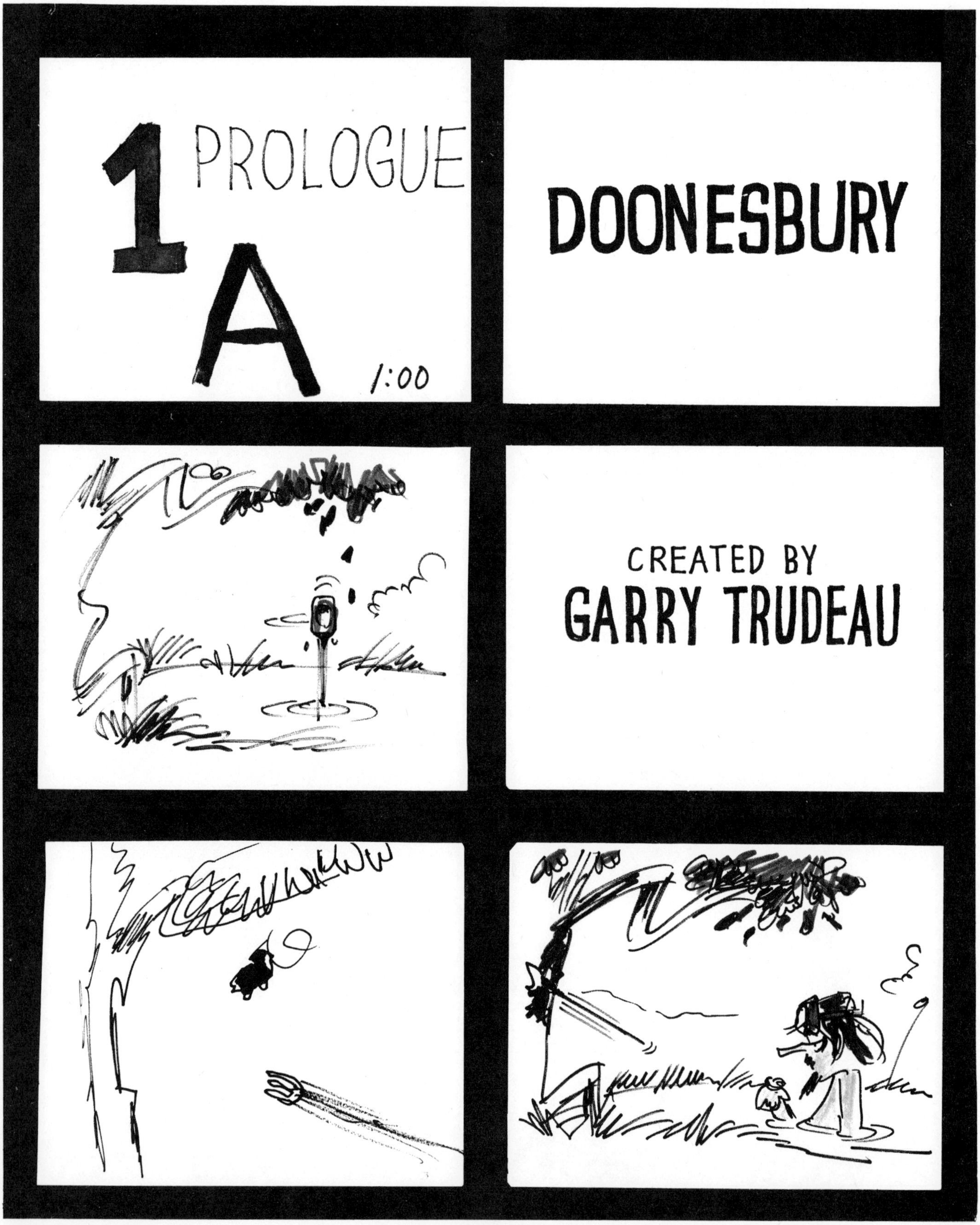
1 PROLOGUE
A
1:00
DOONESBURY
CREATED BY
GARRY TRUDEAU

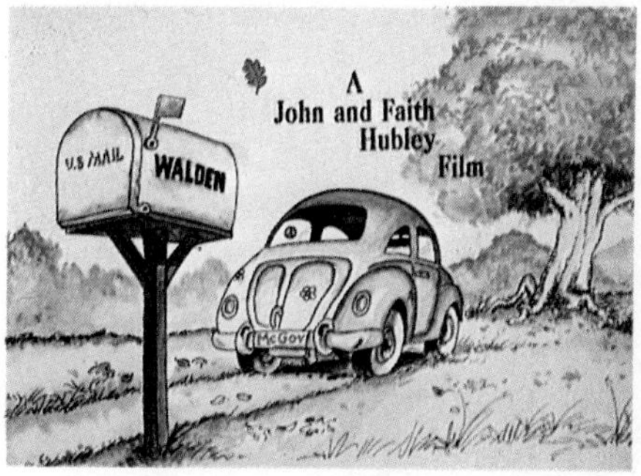
U.S. MAIL
WALDEN
A
John and Faith
Hubley
Film

Pan across Walden Commune foreground. Beat-up VW Beetle with McGovern stickers and daisy stickers parked in front of mailbox. Move down path toward main house, past large, gnarled tree, stopping amd moving in on Walden puddle. Bubbles rising to surface. Frogs croaking, birds chirping.

MIKE

Voice coming from house, off-camera

Zonker! Zonker!

Snorkle breaks surface of pond. Spins, moves slowly in circles, weaving back and forth leaving a trail of bubbles. A solitary leaf is slowly falling through the air, hovering over the puddle.

ZONKER

Steady, lad, steady! That's it...lead it now...that's it...

MIKE

Zonker!

ZONKER

Fire!

Small trident spear breaks the surface of the water, neatly impaling the offending leaf, and lodging in tree trunk near pond. Zonker surfaces to see what he's hit.

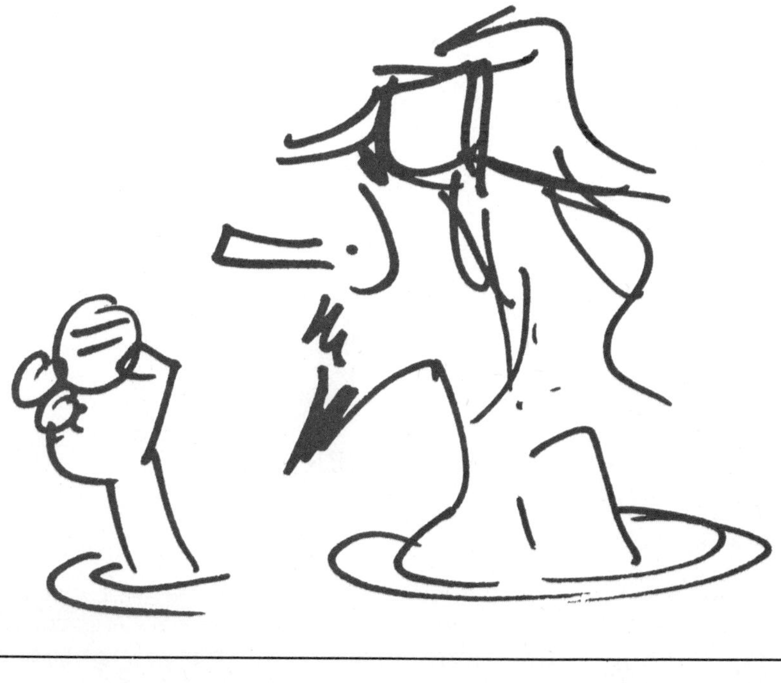

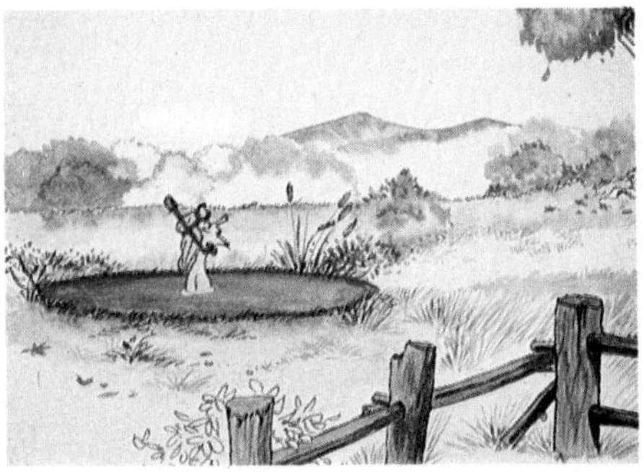

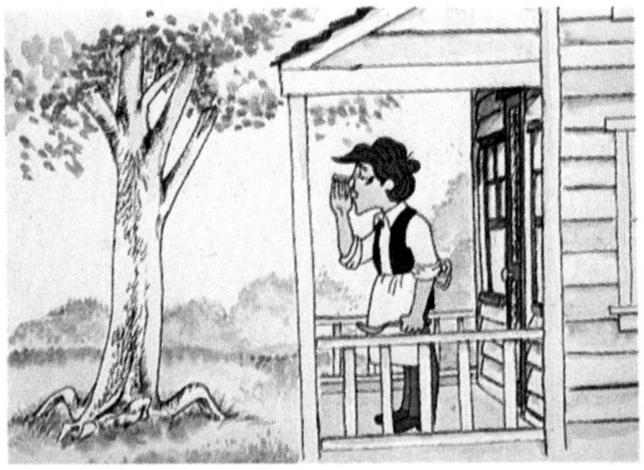

MIKE
Standing on porch of house
Zonker!

ZONKER
What?!

MIKE
Dinner's in ten minutes!

ZONKER
So?

MIKE
We'd prefer you dry.
Disappears back into house

ZONKER
Oh...
Pulls himself out of pond and looks around
Where's my towel?...Towel?...Hello, towel...
Not finding it anywhere nearby, walks toward house.
Zonker enters front door of house and walks into kitchen. He starts going through the cupboards looking for a towel.

ZONKER
Sniffs air
What's that, Mike?

MIKE
Dinner.

ZONKER
Are you sure? Smells like something died.

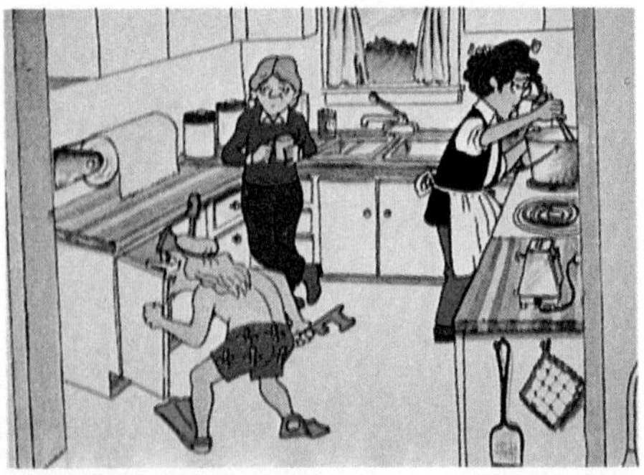

MIKE
Out of here!

ZONKER
I'm gone.
Unable to find a towel, rips up twenty feet of paper towels and heads out of kitchen. Drying hair with towels, walks over to TV set.

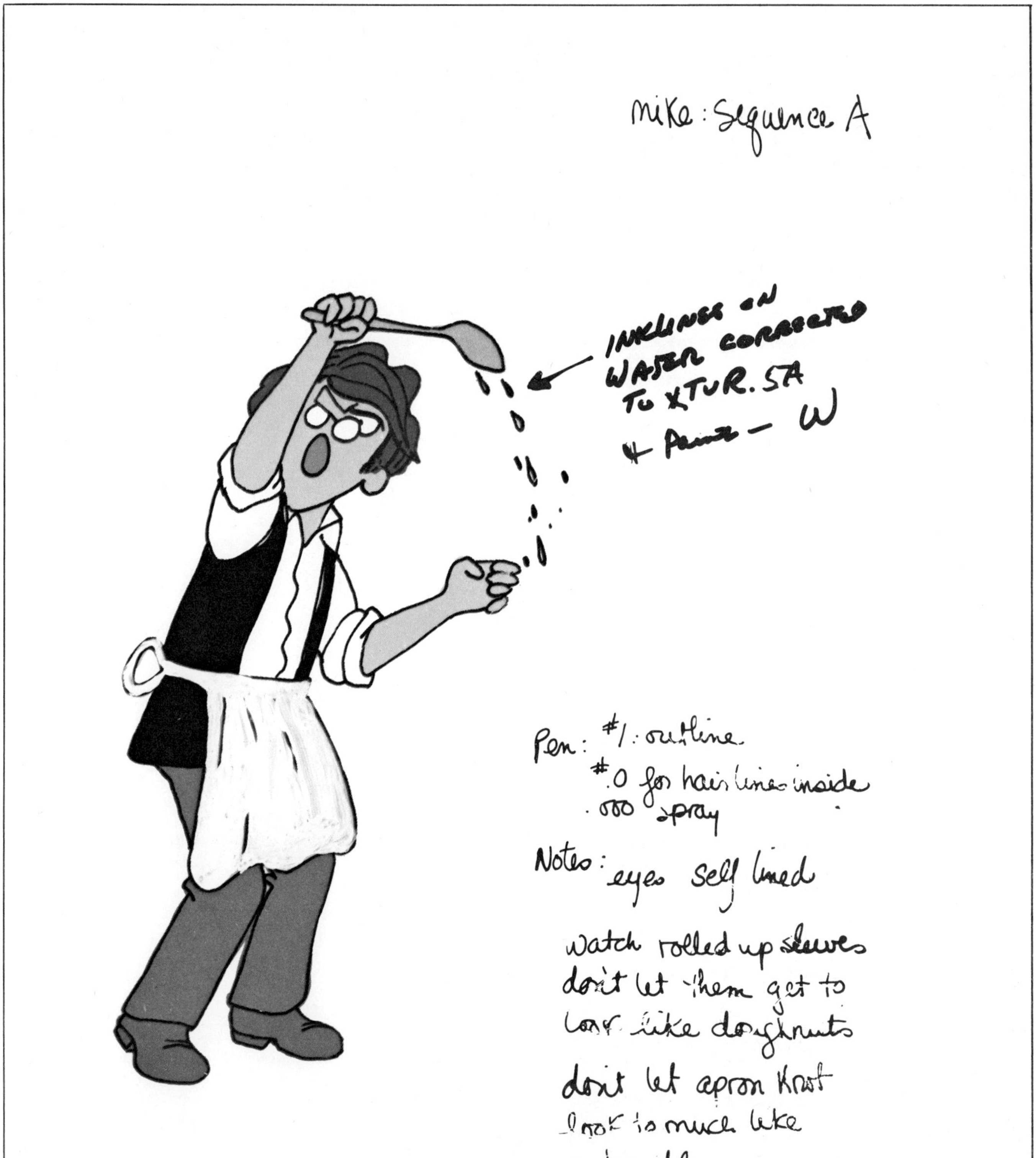

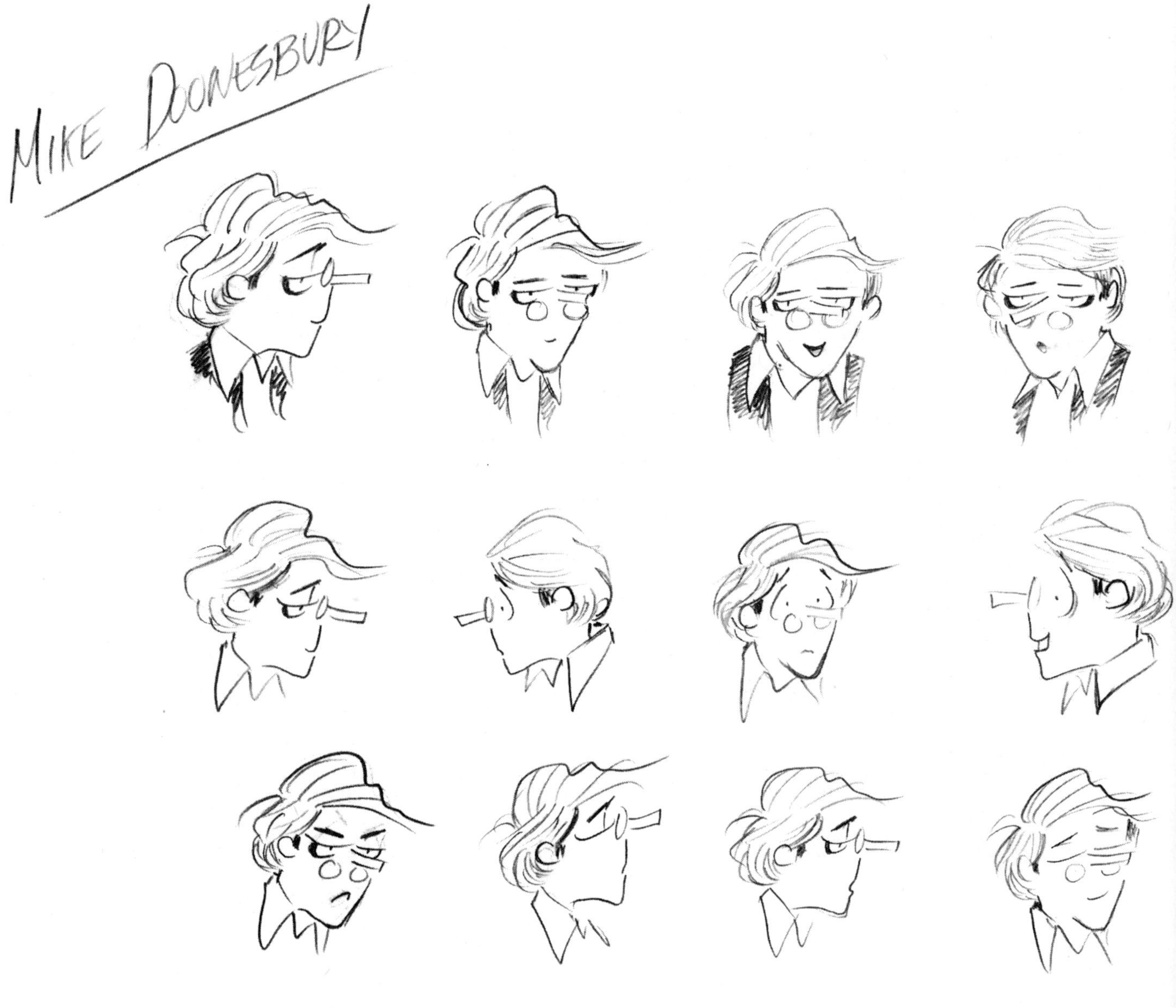
MIKE DOONESBURY

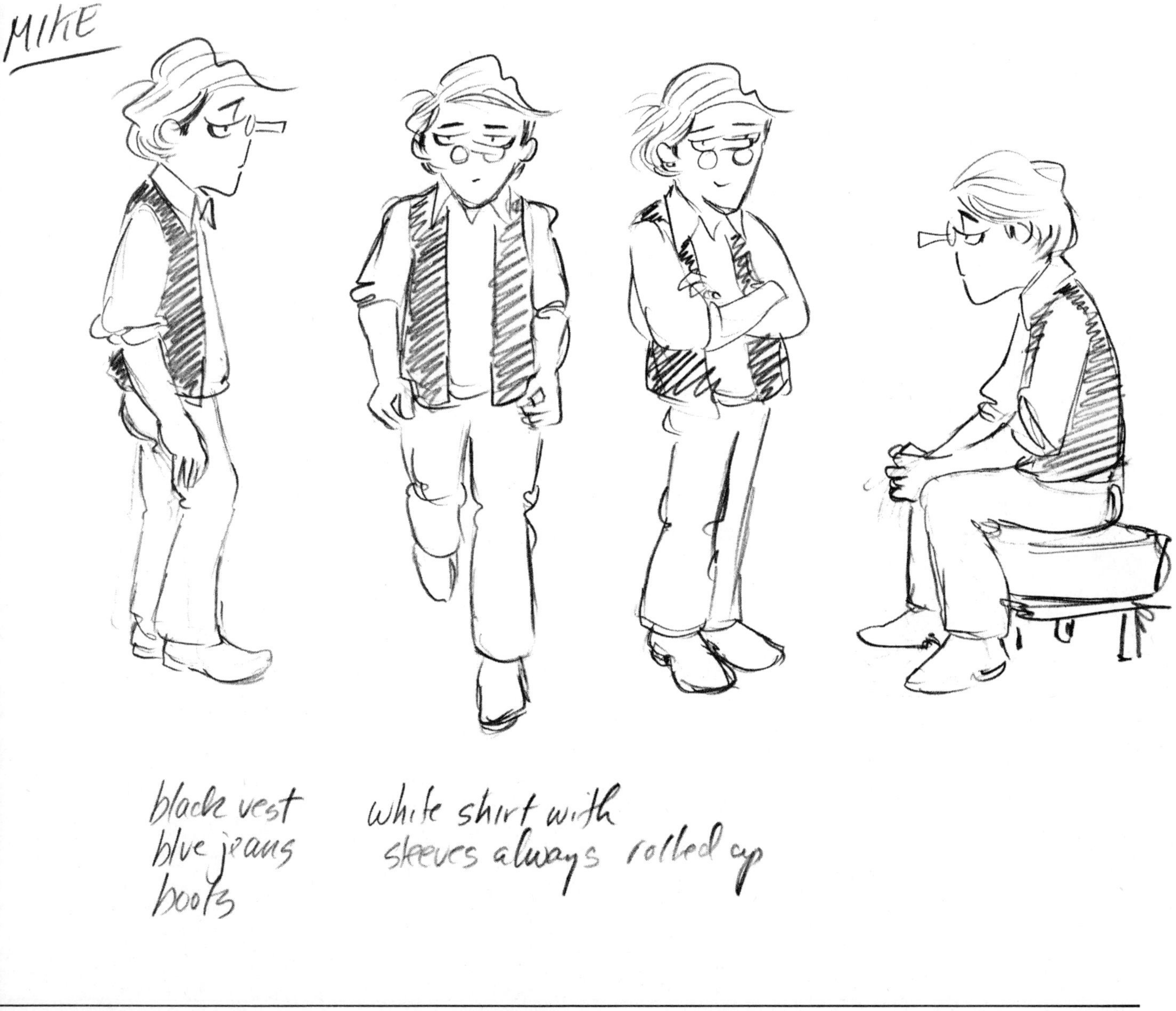
MIKE
black vest
blue jeans
boots
white shirt with
sleeves always rolled up

Zonker sits down in overstuffed sofa in front of the television. He reaches over and turns it on, just in time to catch the very beginning of a Jimmy Thudpucker concert. Camera is on applauding crowd. Applause dies out as we hear director's voice boom over studio monitor.

DIRECTOR

Good! Good! Now, people, I know you're tired, but let's try it one more time, and then we can all get out of here, okay?! Good. Ready? Okay, let's hear it!

Audience erupts into applause and screaming again. Pull back to reveal scene on monitor in control booth, where a half-dozen screens are being watched by the director and his assistant.

DIRECTOR

Tape?

ASSISTANT

Rolling…

DIRECTOR

All right, let's cut this turkey. Cue camera three.

ASSISTANT

You got it.

In tight on one monitor, where we see Jimmy in football shirt sitting at grand piano on stage. He is alone in a single spot as he starts to sing the intro to his song. The act that follows is pure glitter and show biz. The camera work is of the "Midnight Special" variety, with tilts, zooms, split screens, double images, psychedelic color changes. We keep moving in and out of the monitors in the control booth, allowing the very jaded, middle-aged engineers to provide a counterpoint to the electronic, kaleidoscopic images of the musicians onstage. On occasion, we pull back farther to see Zonker watching the engineers watching.

Lyrics for "Stop in the Middle"
THUDPUCKER

sings
Hello, yes, it's me.
I heard you on the air.
You spoke of foreign wars,
And how you used to care.

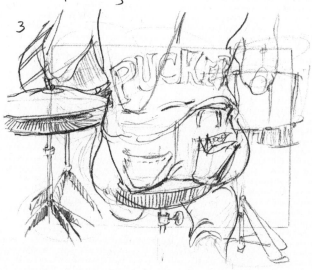

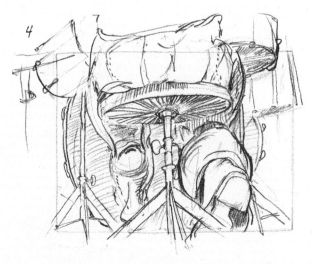

1

2

opening shot: High view of drummer with effect of zooming in and panning.

3

4

panning continues until drummer is perpendicular.

from point slightly below seat we begin trucking in

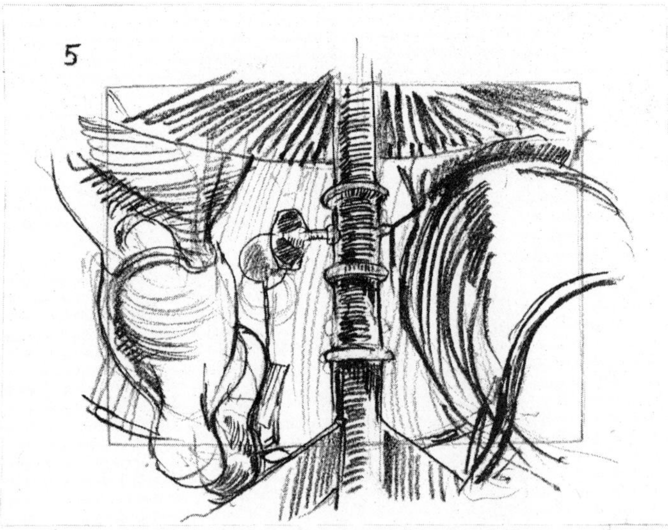
5

continue trucking toward Bass Drum

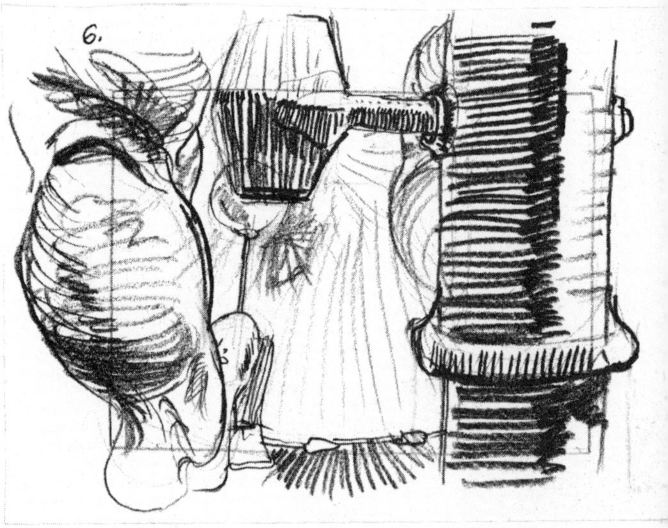
6.

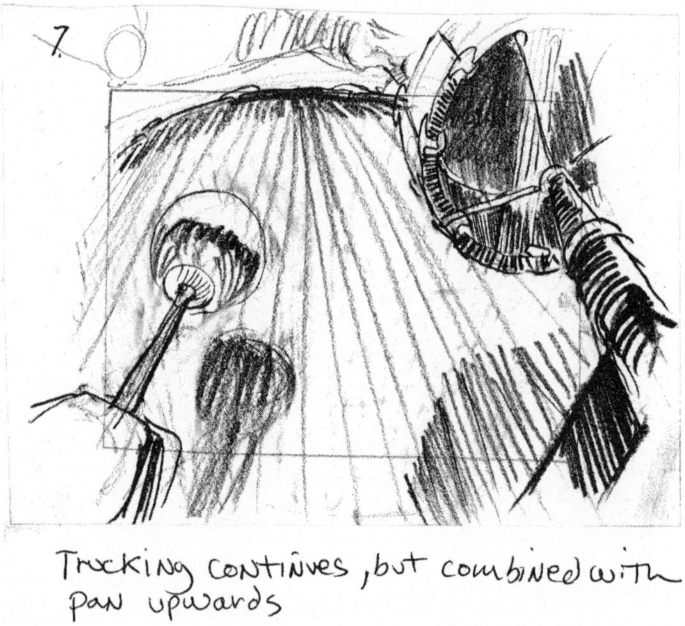
7.

Trucking continues, but combined with pan upwards

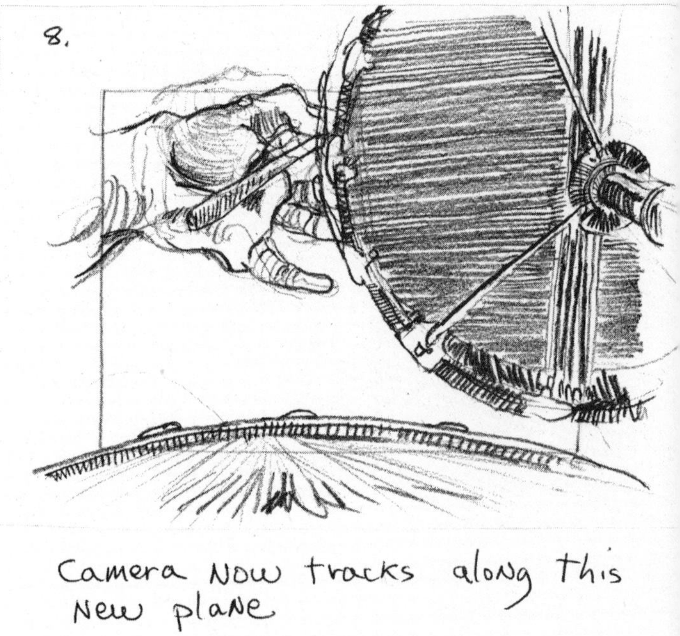
8.

Camera now tracks along this new plane

9.

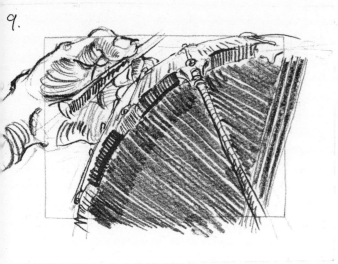

10.

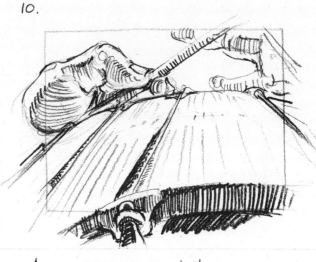

As camera passes bottom of snare drum it begins to slowly pan

11.

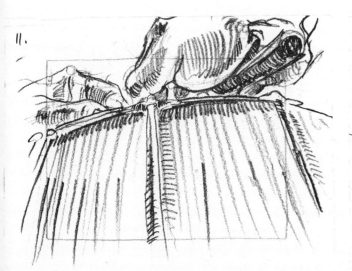

12.

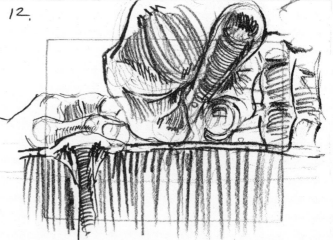

Both hands now clearly visible. Panning continues

Pan almost complete as camera crests the top of drum.

13

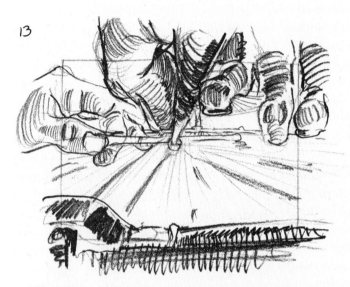

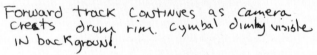

Forward track continues as camera crests drum rim. cymbal dimly visible in background.

14

Camera continues track beneath drummers right hand as he beats

15

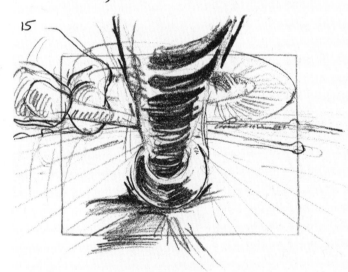

Drum stick pounces down in our path as beat continues

16.

cymbal now clearly visible

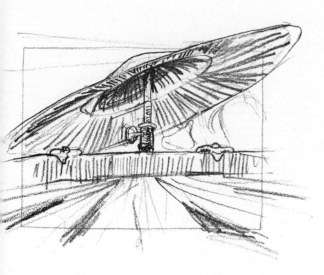

18

Guitarist moves into view behind
Cymbal

20

microphone visible for a moment
guitarist almost in center. Guitar
rift begins

guitarist raises guitar. audience
dimly indicated

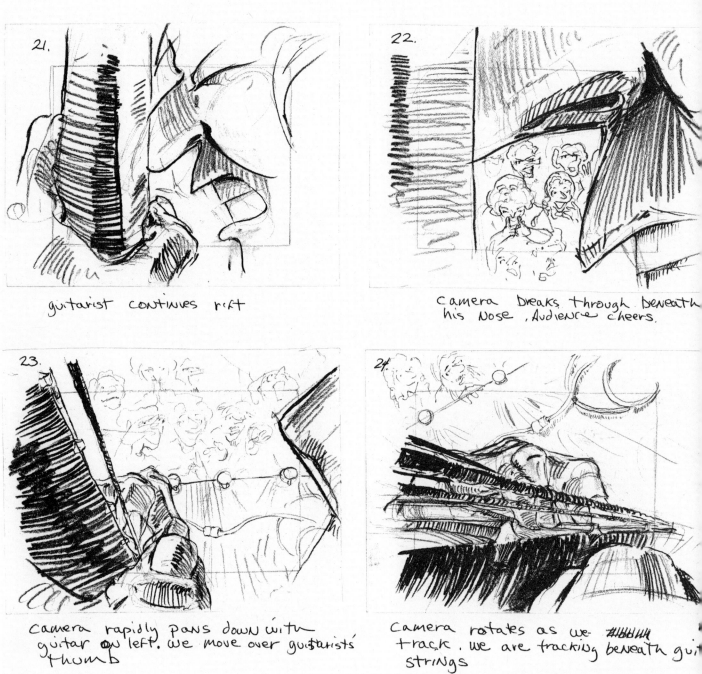

21. guitarist continues rift

22. camera breaks through beneath his nose. Audience cheers.

23. camera rapidly pans down with guitar on left. we move over guitarists' thumb

24. Camera rotates as we ######## track. we are tracking beneath guitar strings

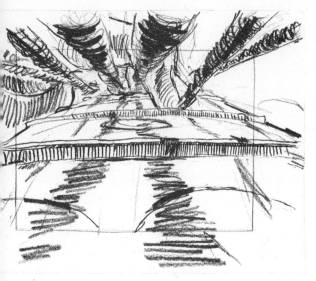

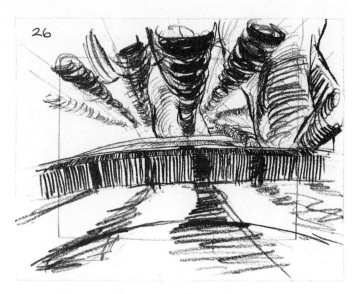

station continues until camera centers
on deck of guitar, fingers manipulate
strings

just clearing the frets we track
down between guitarists fingers

rotating with edge of ring finger
camera heads for light

29

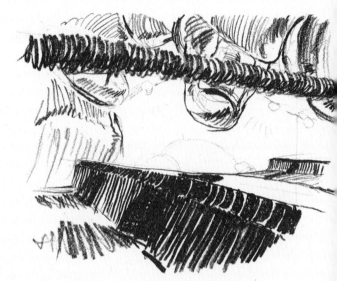

passing ~~now~~ now beneath last two strings

As view expands, stage is now vis below.

31

clearing the edge of the guitar audience again visible

32

camera swoops down to audience as it gesticulates

I wouldn't want to hold you
To words of way back when,
But now is not so very far from then.

Stop in the middle of your life for asking,
Who came of age with youthful rage at My Lai?
Stop in the middle of your life,
Take another look at the wayward fight.
Stop and remember what the winds of change were like.

One more chance for breathing,
One more chance for change.
Just let it in and let it out like Jude.
Each moment had its movement,
Each movement had its day,
But I'm still a friend who cares enough to say…

Stop in the middle of your life for asking,
When, where, why, who and what became of you?
Stop in the middle of your life,
Take another look at the wayward fight.
Stop and remember what the winds of change were like.

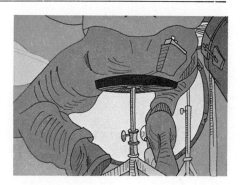

*The song finally ends amidst tumultuous applause. Director leans forward
in chair, turns off sound.*

DIRECTOR
Sighs
I can live with it. Let 'em go.
See you Monday.
As he gets up, flicks off monitor with Zonker still peering out of it.

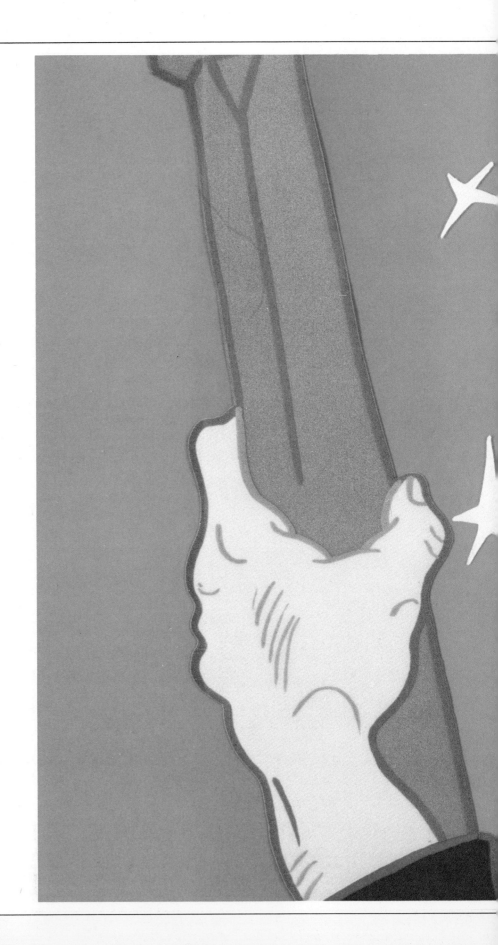

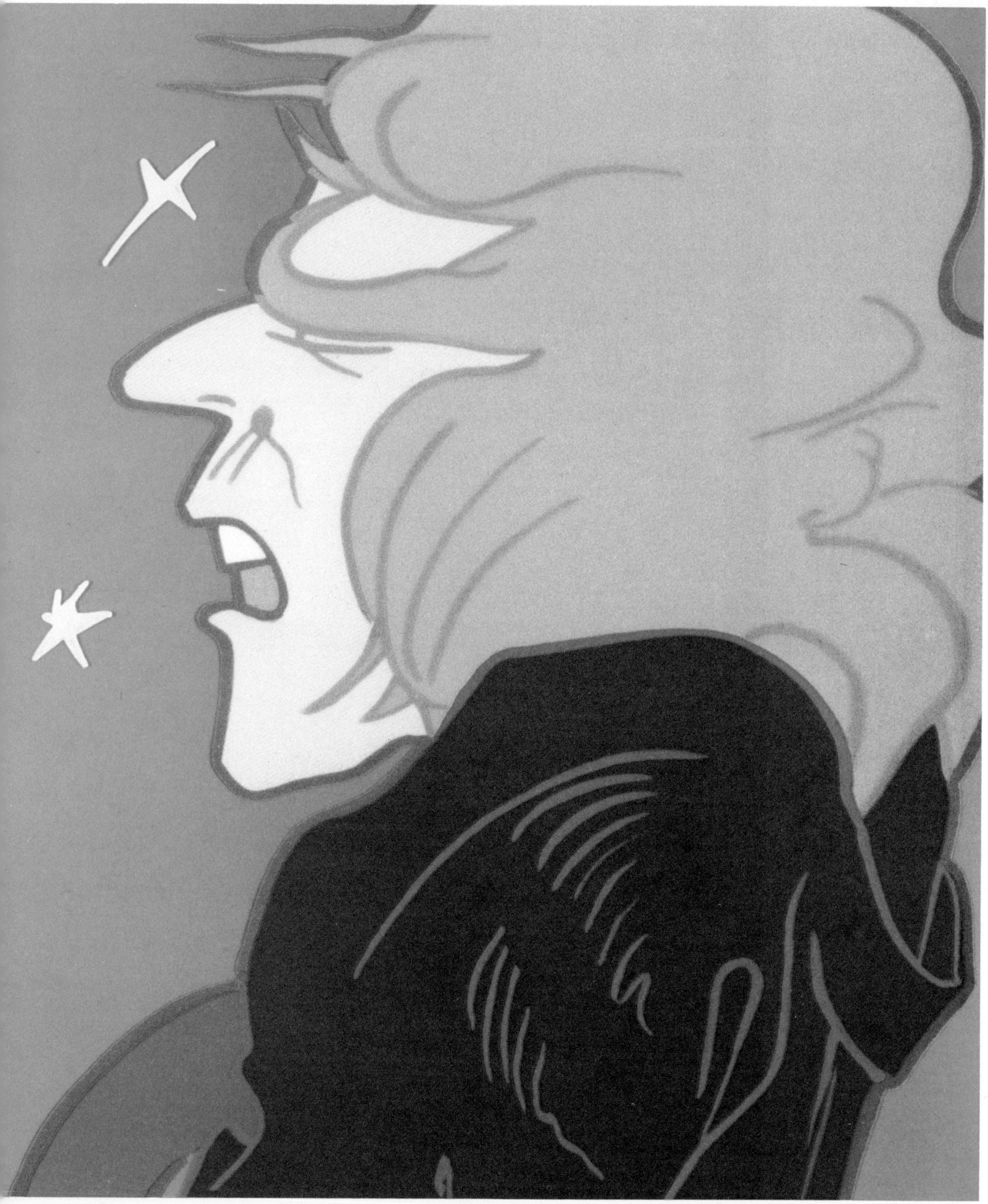

Open on Zonker's flippered feet at the top of the staircase. As he descends the stairs, we pull back to see Zonker rehearsing a speech. He is immaculate and beautiful. His hair is freshly blow-dried, and he is dressed in white tie, tails, and neatly pressed surfing jams. We hear the voices of the other members of the house coming from the dining room.

ZONKER

I'd like to thank you all for being here....It's a wonderful turnout and I certainly appreciate that...you're a beautiful bunch of...cats...
Words turn into mumbling as the voice level of dinner conversation comes up. Zonker enters the dining room. Absolutely no one notices.

MARK

Poking at food
Mike. I gotta ask you. Is this stuff benign?

MIKE

Well, of course, it is! What kind of...

B.D.

Does it have a name, Mike? Does the meal in front of us have a name?

BOOPSIE

This really is the strangest-tasting dish, Michael.

B.D.

Mike, did it come in a can, or did it just follow you home?

MARK

Now, Joanie, this is really your responsibility. You know Mike needs supervision when...

JOANIE

I know and I'm sorry. I only left the room for a second and...
Zonker is moving about the room. By now he has set up a lectern at his place at the table, attached a microphone to it, plugged the cord into an amp, and is adjusting his reading light.

MIKE

Look, all right! So I tried something different...

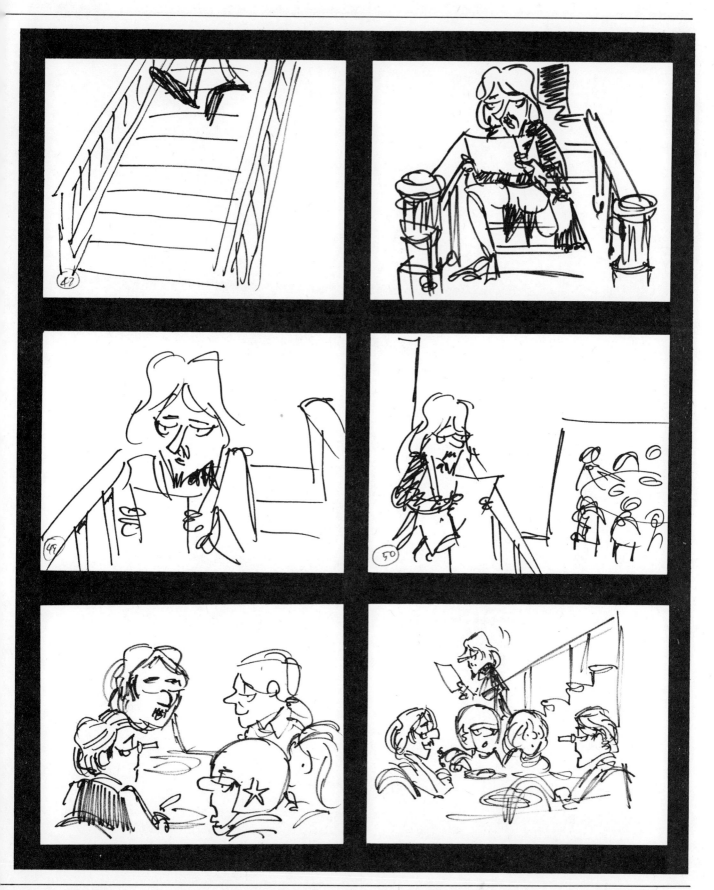

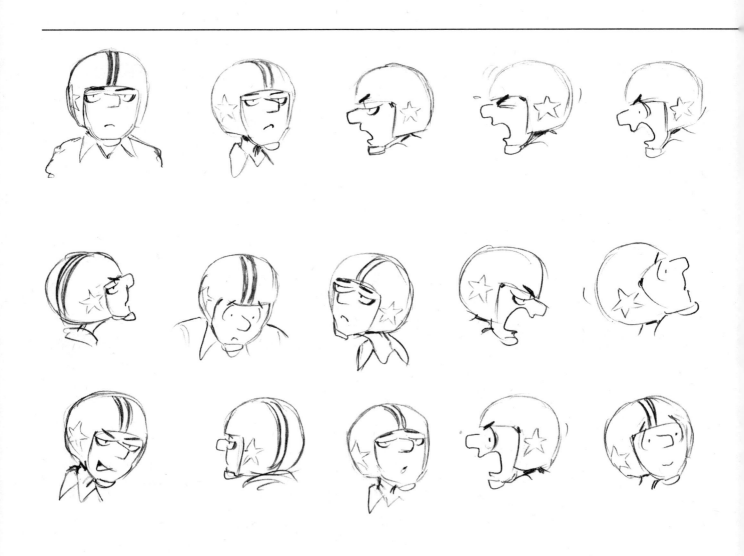

ZONKER
Testing mike
Test! Test! One, two, one, two.

MARK
It moved. I think…I…just saw it move.

MIKE
Oh, for…Look! It's lasagna! It's just plain ol'…

MARK
With delight
I did! It's eating my peas!

BOOPSIE
Jeepers! It is! It is!

ZONKER
Ready to go, trying to get everyone's attention
Ahem! Ahem!

B.D.
Where'd you get the recipe, Mike? Sports Illustrated?

MIKE
Look, Mark! I don't claim to be a great chef. I'm just a regular guy trying to get some food on the table…

ZONKER
Getting annoyed
Hello? Hello?
Starts tapping Mike's wineglass

MIKE
Now, if that doesn't suit you, you all know where the Colonel is, so you can…
Zonker keeps hitting Mike's wineglass, until finally it shatters. Everyone stops talking and notices Zonker for the first time.

MARK
Would you like to say something, Zonker?

ZONKER

Yes. I would like to thank everyone for being here for the fourth annual State of the Commune Address…

Groans from everyone

JOANIE

State of the what?

MIKE

Oh, god, not again…

ZONKER

It's a wonderful turnout and I certainly appreciate that. Now, I don't want to take up too much of your time tonight, so I'm going to skip over the perennial problems and issues, cut through all the damn clichés and get down to brass tacks!

MARK

Hear! Hear!

B.D.

Sum up! Sum up!

ZONKER

You got it. Here's the essence of my message tonight, the nugget, the grain, if you will, the hard kernel of truth, as bitter as it may be to swallow…

Long pause, as everyone leans forward

Communal living is passé.

MIKE

What!

ZONKER

End of message. End of state-of-commune message.

BOOPSIE

Passé?

B.D.

To Boopsie

That is not exactly a hot flash.

MARK
Where will I go? Who will I be? What will I eat?

ZONKER

Those are good questions, Markus. Because unless you're Chinese, the commune's had it. There's just been too dramatic a shift in our social needs and interests. For example, how long has it been since any of us has been into organic gardening, or macramé, or even group sex?

JOANIE
Yes, it has been a while.

MARK
Yeah, I think I see what you're driving at, Zonk…

ZONKER
Now then. I propose that we all disband, intermarry and move into condominiums.
Everyone chokes, drops silverware, etc.

MIKE
Condominiums?!

MARK
Campers! I think we should start with campers!

B.D.
Scratching his nose
Yeah, Chevy makes a pretty good one.

MIKE
Genuinely alarmed
CONDOMINIUMS!? Are you out of your mind?

ZONKER
Thank you. You've been beautiful. Enjoy the show.
Mixture of applause, catcalls, laughter follow as Zonker flicks off the mike switch and ceremoniously leaves the room.

ZONKER

ZONKER

BLUE JEANS
T-SHIRT w. STAR IN CENTER
BOOTS

B.D.
Getting up with look of disgust on his face
Gross. Gross speech, gross meal. C'mon Boopsie, game's starting on the
tube.

BOOPSIE
Standing up, folding napkin, to Mike
Thank you, Mike, your dinner was very…colorful.
*Mark is still laughing to himself. As Boopsie and B.D. go into kitchen,
Joanie starts to clear table. Mark finally notices that Mike is brooding.*

MARK
Hey! What's the matter with you?

MIKE
He was serious, you know. He wasn't kidding.

MARK
About the condominiums? Oh, come on…

MIKE
No, no, just about…you know…the passage of an era.

MARK
Well, yeah…I mean, events and stuff…they're different. But not our con-
cerns, our priorities…the basics…

MIKE
The basics?

MARK
Yeah, you know…the things worth fighting for…

MIKE
When was the last time we fought for anything?

MARK
Aaah, you're being literal.

MIKE
The same question applies figuratively. I mean…when we started out
here…we had an energy…. Remember? And it took so many forms…

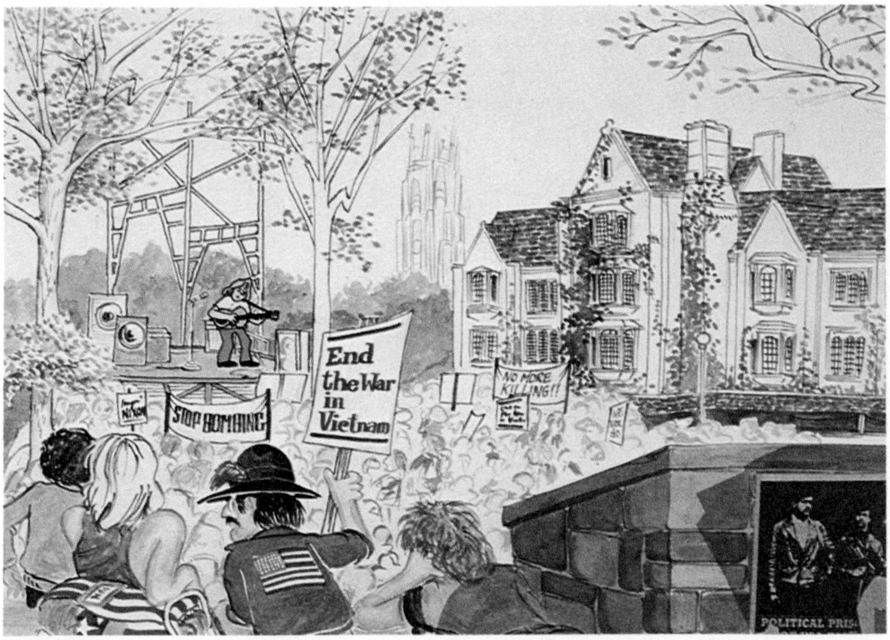
End the War in Vietnam
STOP BOMBING
NO MORE KILLING!!
NIXON

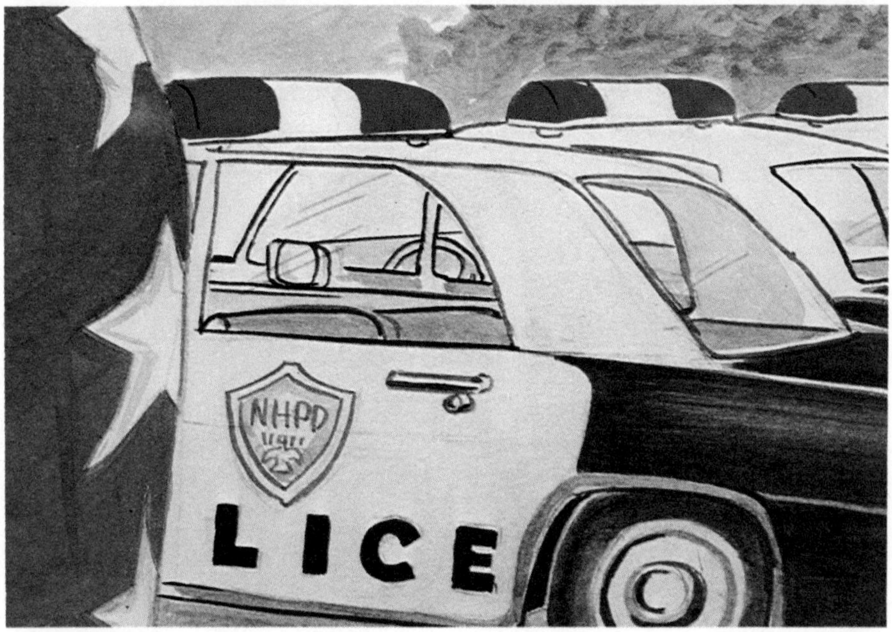
NHPD
LICE

MARK

Smiling to himself

Yeah...remember the moratorium...

MIKE

Ah, the peace concert!

Beat

Jimmy Thudpucker!

MARK

Right. Back when he was the callowest of fellows.

Reaches over to record collection beneath stereo

Still got that one...

Mark puts on record, sits back on couch with Mike as scratchy music comes on. As they listen, the scene transforms into an outdoor peace demonstration in the early seventies.

Most of the main characters—Mike, Mark, Zonker, Scot, and Boopsie—are seated on the grass watching Jimmy Thudpucker play. The scene is in marked contrast to Jimmy's earlier glitter appearance. The song is a troubadour's ode to peace and harmony and antiwar sentiment in general. It has an anthem quality to it, and the hundred or so people in the audience join with him on the choruses. The mood is carefree and upbeat; even the National Guard who are stationed near the back of the crowd seem to be having a good time. The blinkers on top of the squad cars are keeping time with the music.

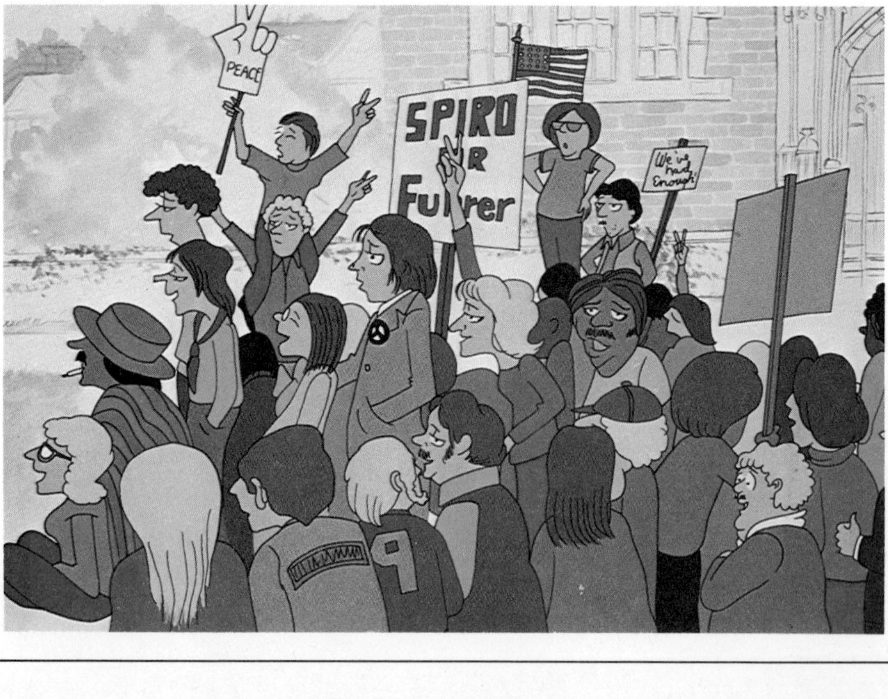
PEACE
SPIRO
We've had Enough!

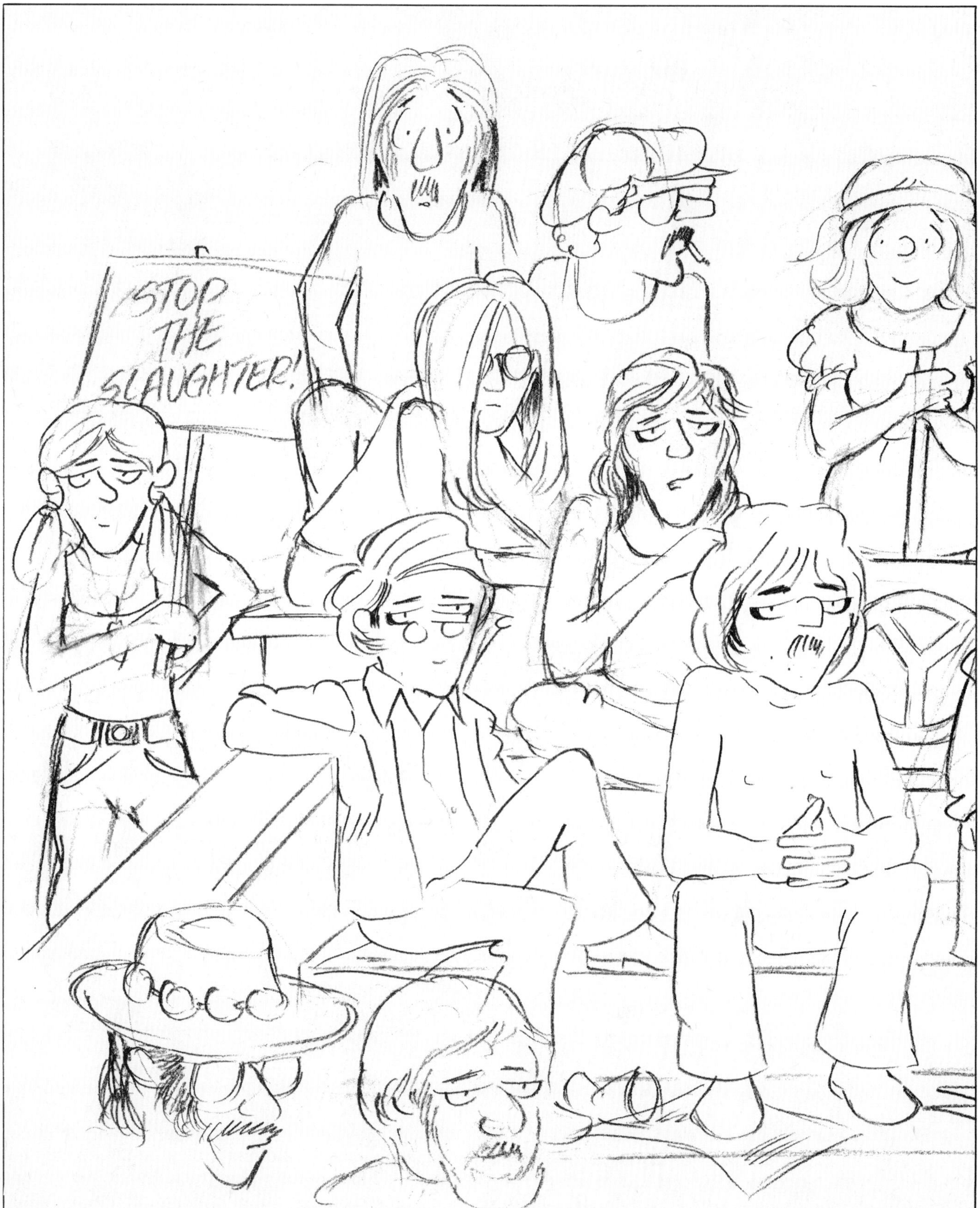
STOP THE SLAUGHTER!

white skin : Flesh #15
Black skin : Sun Flesh #17
uniform : Tan #10
helmets }
belts   } olive Drab #20

Tear gas Can }
gun barrels } grey #7

Cap on Can : grey #18

boots : grey #32

Club
gun stocks } brown #19

eyes — white

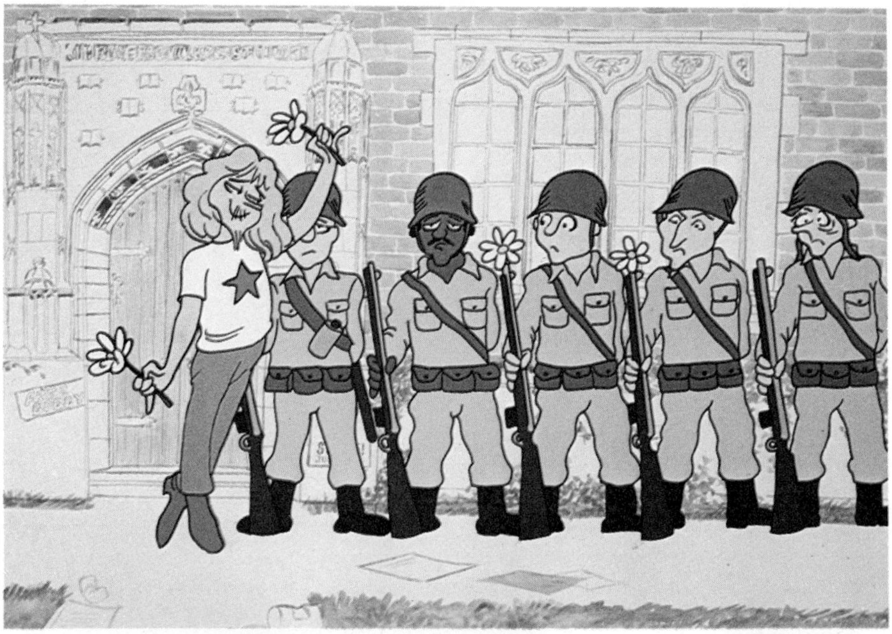

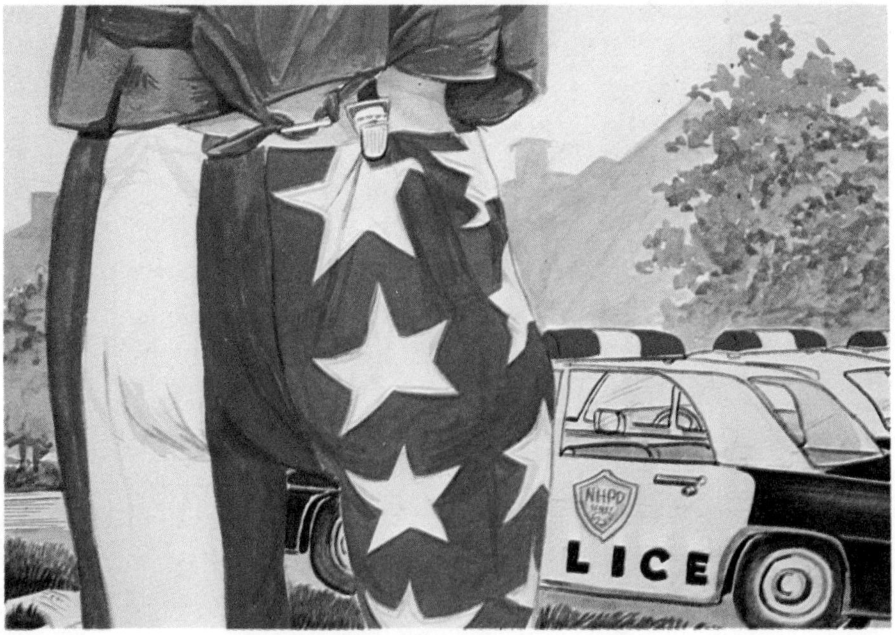
NHPD
LICE

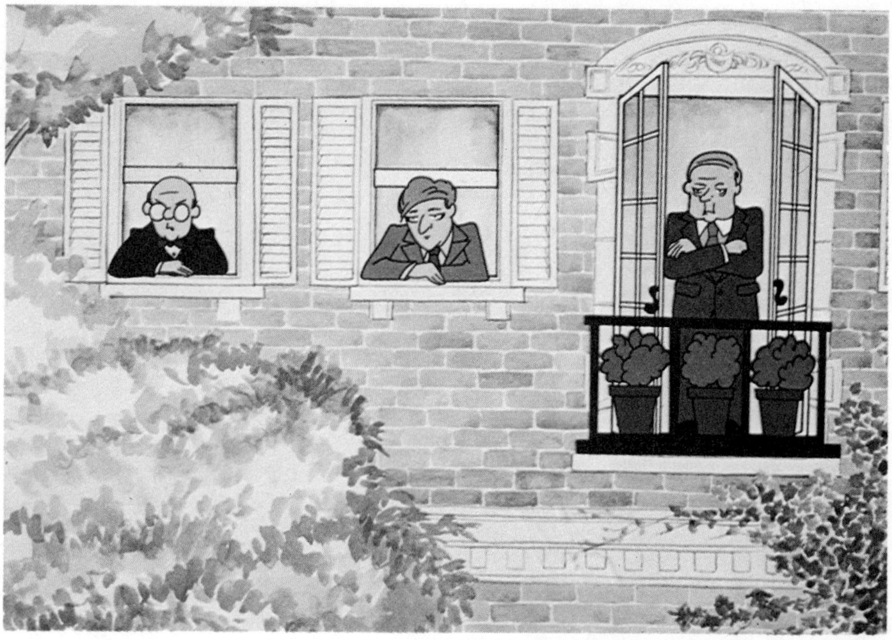

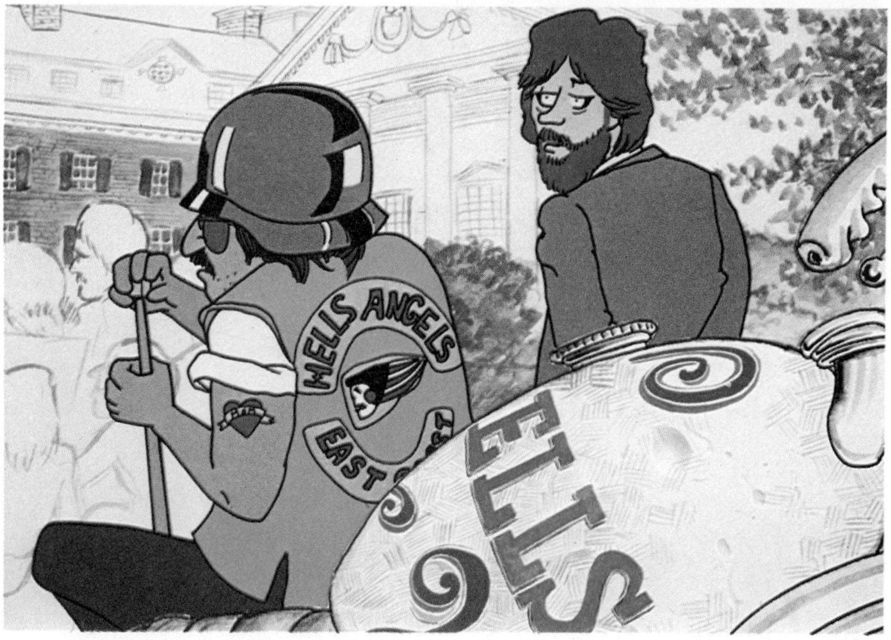
HELLS ANGELS
EAST

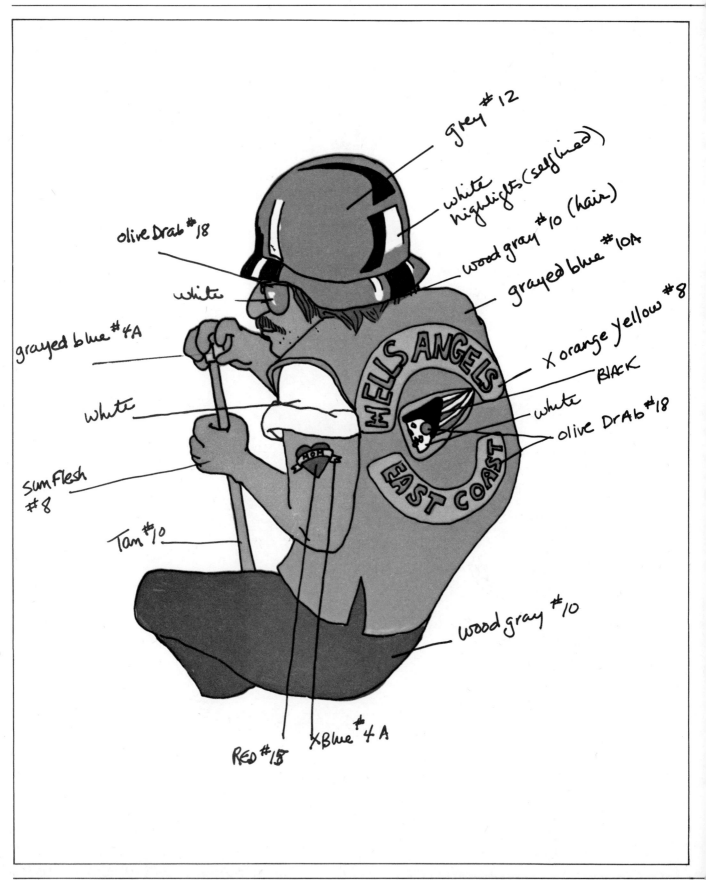

grey #12

white highlights (selflined)

wood gray #10 (hair)

grayed blue #10A

olive Drab #18

white

grayed blue #4A

white

SumFlesh #8

Tan #10

X orange Yellow #8

BLACK

white

olive DrAb #18

WELLS ANGELS

EAST COAST

wood gray #10

RED #18

XBlue #4A

Lyrics for "I Do Believe"
THUDPUCKER
Sings
I do believe, yes, I do believe
A day will come
When all mankind
Will take the time
To understand.
I do believe, yes, I do believe
The peace we'll find
Will multiply itself in us
Until the end of time.

Some say they know the story's over.
They say the end is nearing now
If only we could stop…and think it over.
And try to touch each others' lives somehow.

The mood is broken when halfway through the song, a rookie National Guardsman, while adjusting his equipment, maces himself by mistake and starts flailing out at everyone around him. The chain of events, thereafter, follows the classic confrontation tradition—chanting, rock throwing, tear gassing, and night sticking—all held in perfect counterpoint by Jimmy Thudpucker's love-and-peace anthem, which he continues to sing in apparent unawareness of the ongoing contradiction. As the end of the song approaches, local football star, B.D., and fellow jocks come to the rescue of the overtaxed National Guard. A particularly overzealous Guardsman, missing his intended target, inadvertently bashes B.D. in the knee with his night stick, just as the song ends.

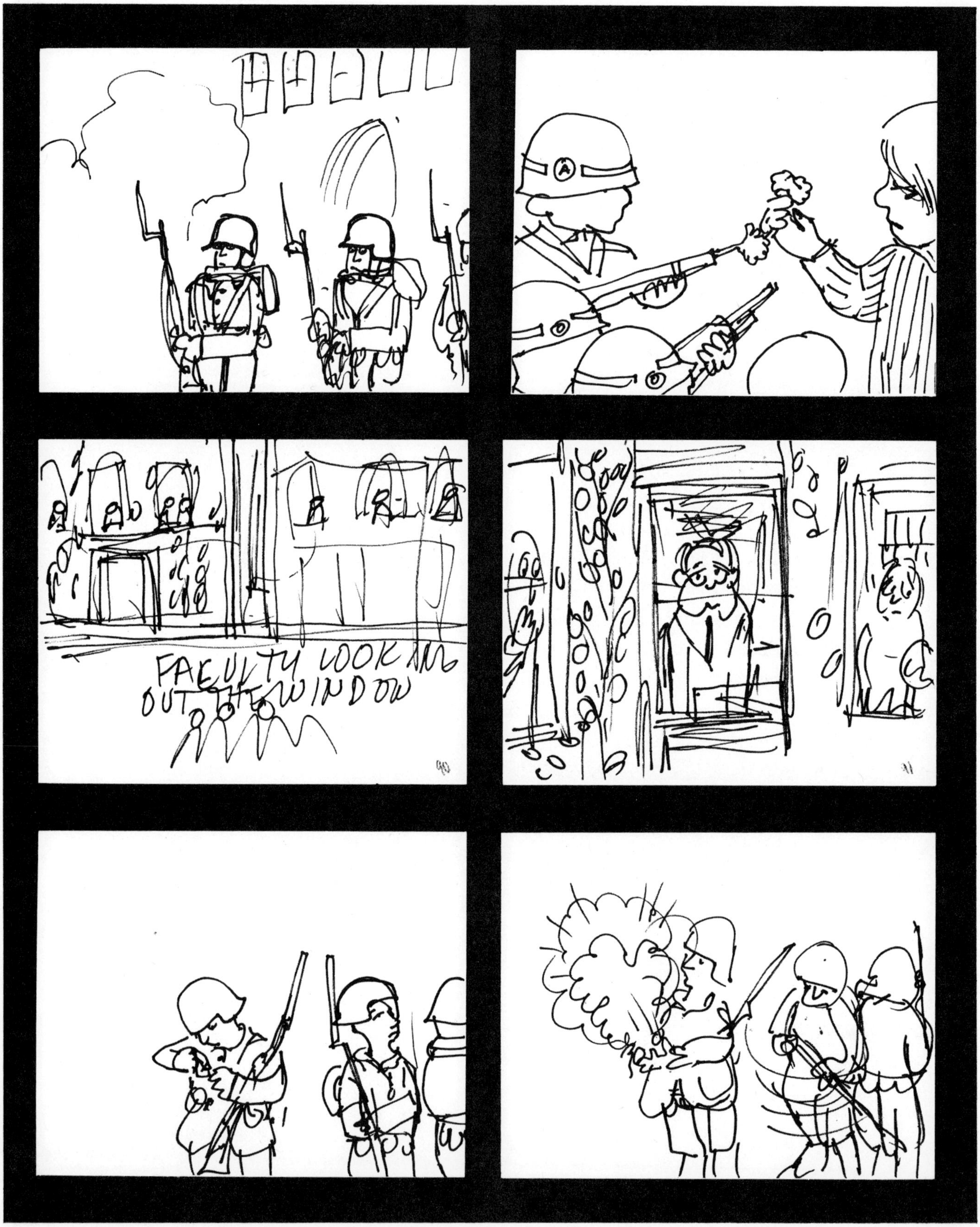
FACULTY LOOKING
OUT THE WINDOW

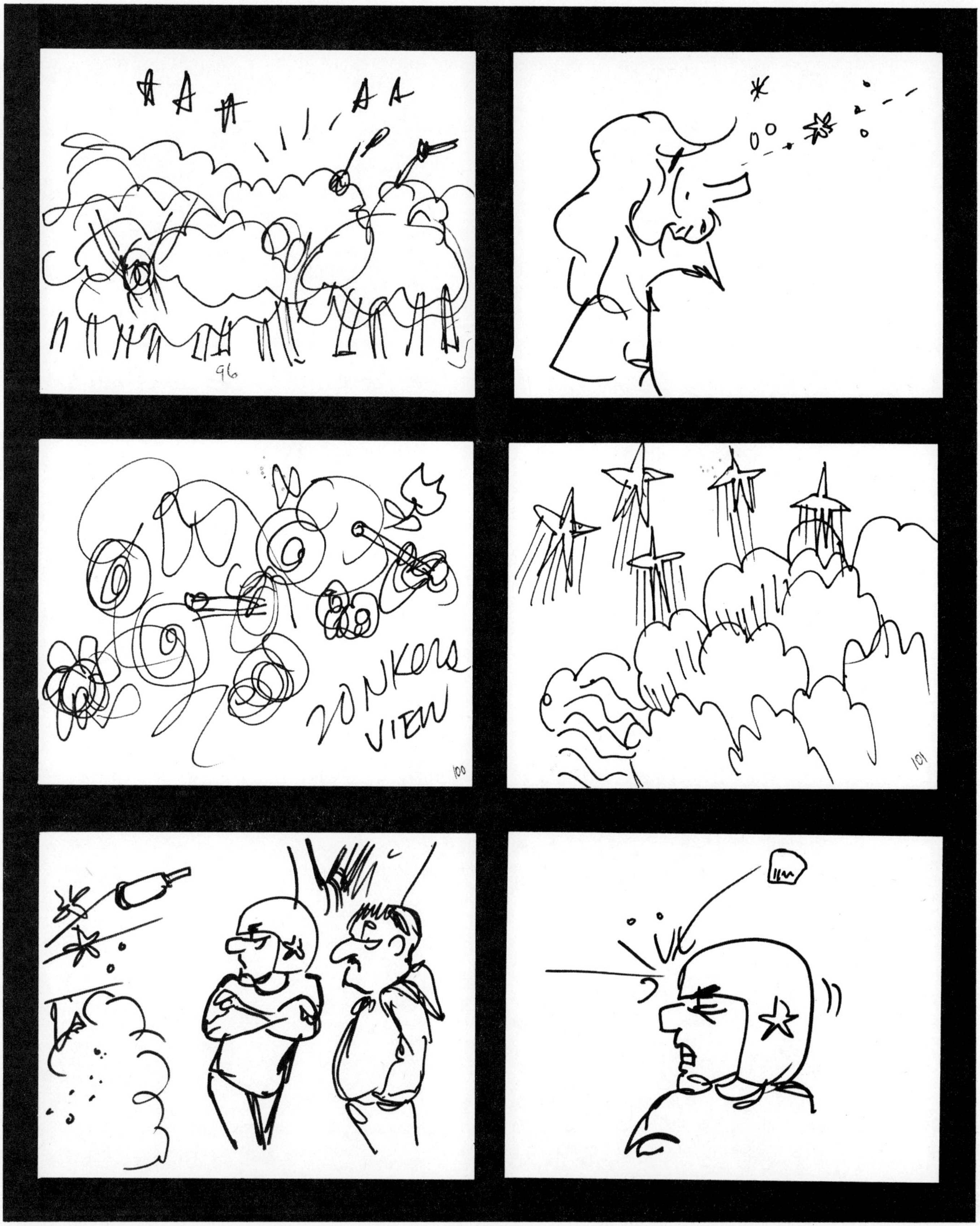
96
ZONKERS
VIEW
100
101

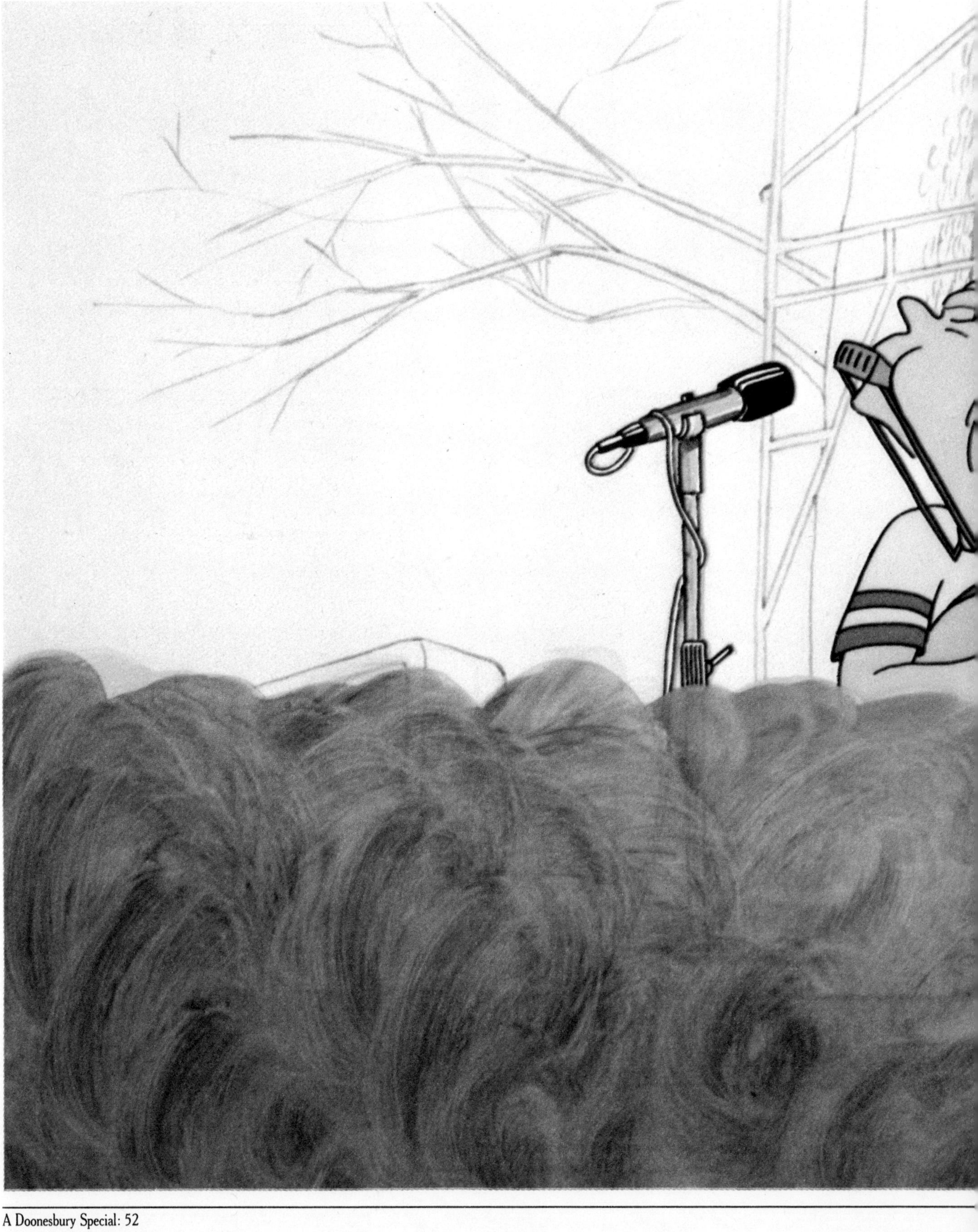

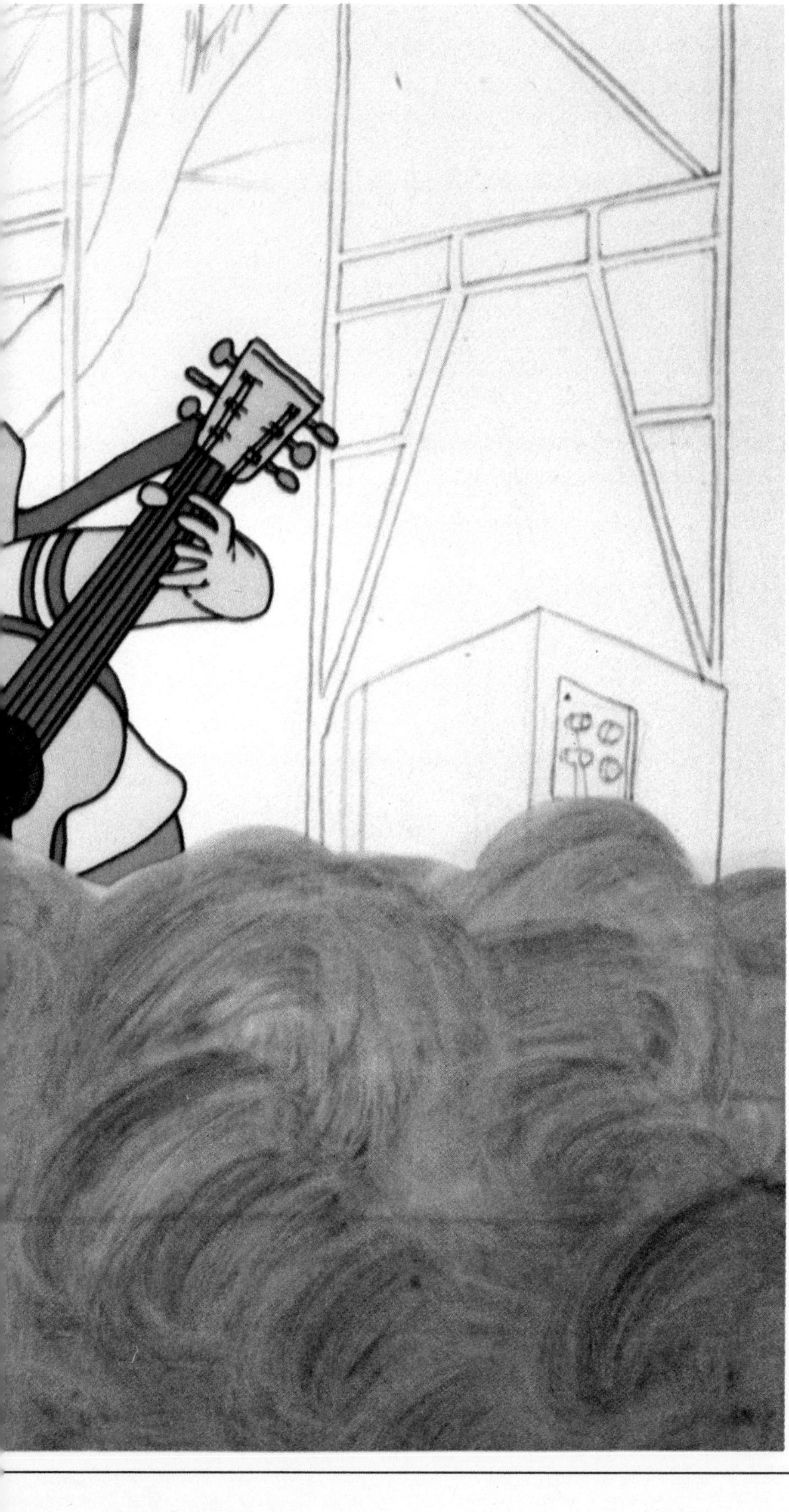

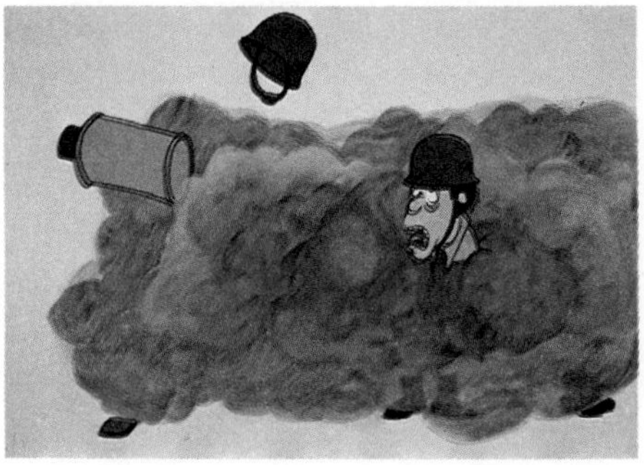

Cut to B.D. bandaging his knee in the locker room.
Tight shot of B.D.'s knee. Pull back to see B.D., Zonker, and Kirby in deserted locker room. All are in full-dress football gear.

ZONKER
Oh, my, what a nasty bruise! See that, Kirby, let that be a lesson to you!

KIRBY
Okay. What?

ZONKER
Violence begets violence!

KIRBY
Well, I'd heard that.

ZONKER
And let that be a lesson to you, Cap'n! Vigilantism is the last refuge of a scoundrel.

B.D.
Getting up and starting to hobble toward door
Drop dead, Harris.

ZONKER
Now, don't be like that, Cap'n. If ever there was a need for dialogue, it's now. Before it's too late. For me. For you. For your many admirers.
B.D., Kirby, and Zonker start to walk through tunnel.

B.D.
Look, I don't want to talk about it! We've got a football game to play!

ZONKER
All the more reason to talk about it, Cap'n! Don't you see? Football itself, with all its violence, has become a grotesque metaphor for American aggression in Indochina!

B.D.
That's ridiculous!

KIRBY
Zonker, are you suggesting a parallel between interventionalism and contact sports?

1

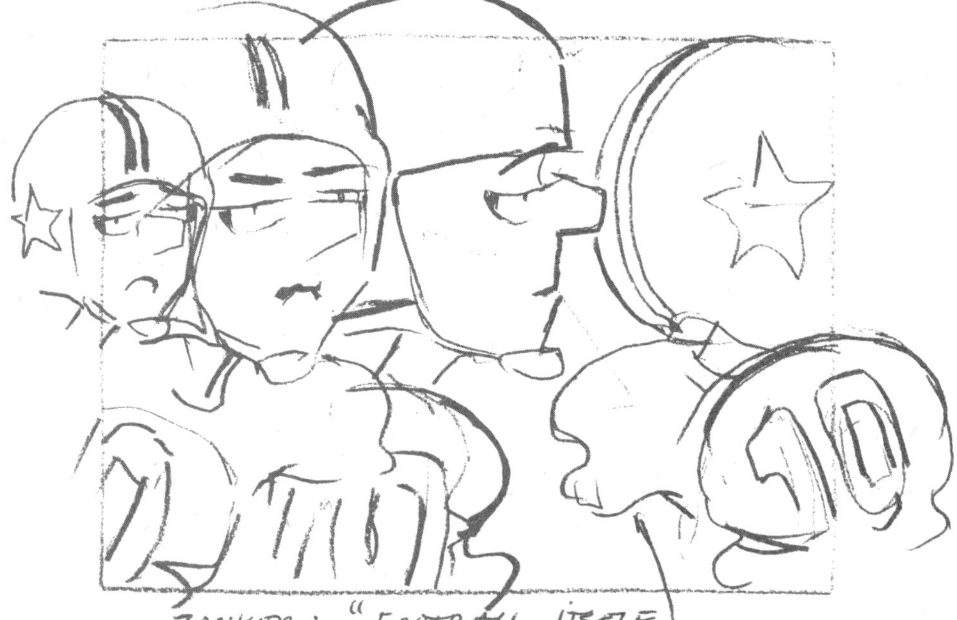

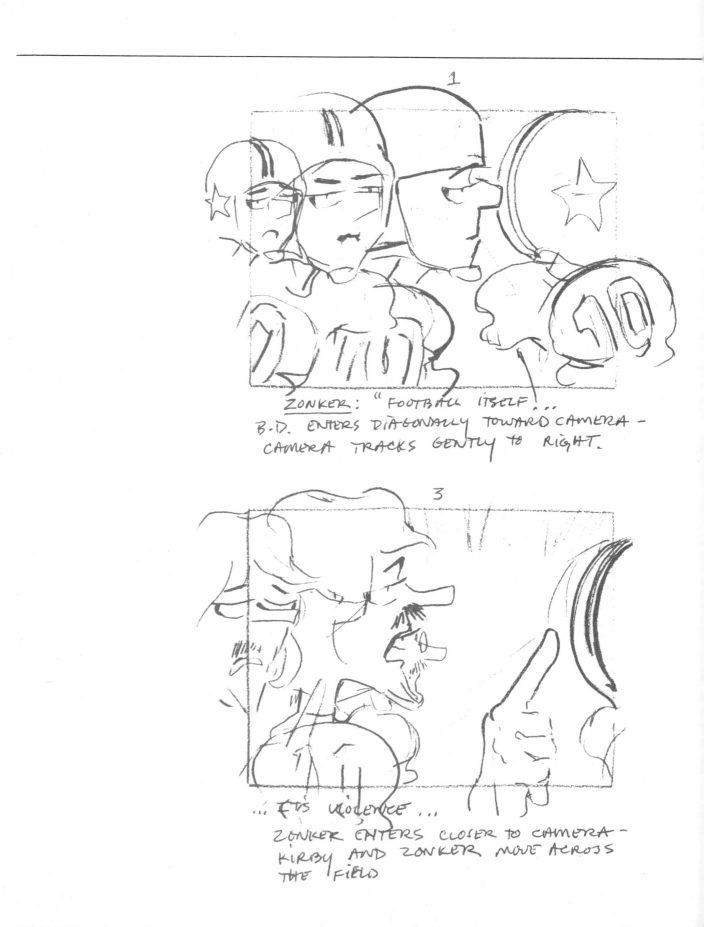

ZONKER: "FOOTBALL ITSELF...
B.D. ENTERS DIAGONALLY TOWARD CAMERA - CAMERA TRACKS GENTLY TO RIGHT.

3

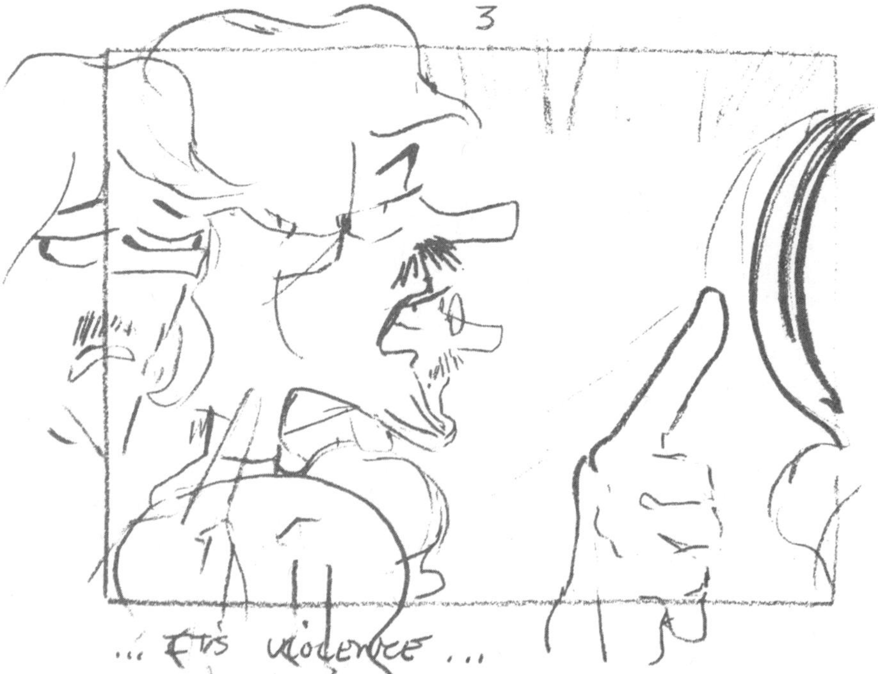

... ITS VIOLENCE ...
ZONKER ENTERS CLOSER TO CAMERA - KIRBY AND ZONKER MOVE ACROSS THE FIELD

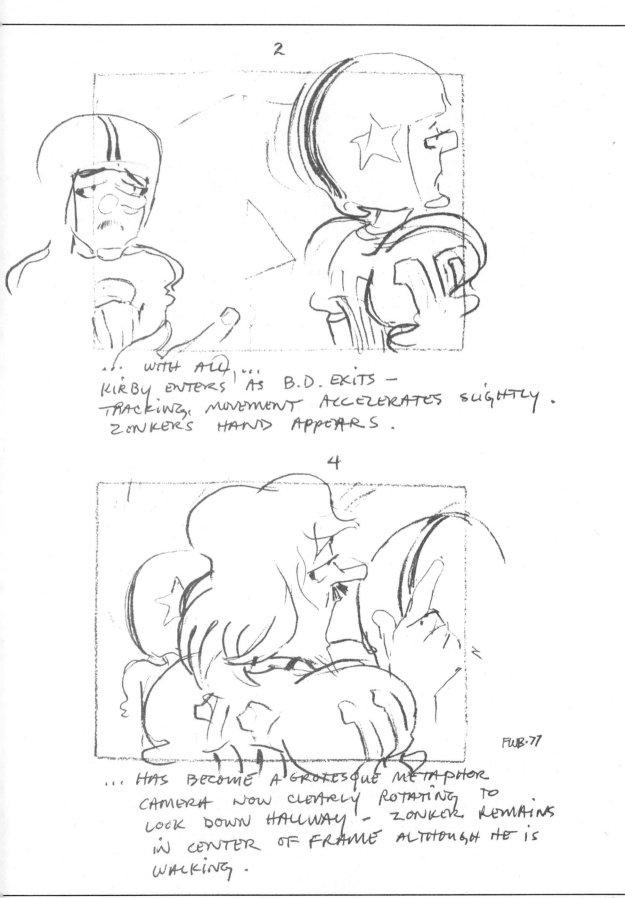

2

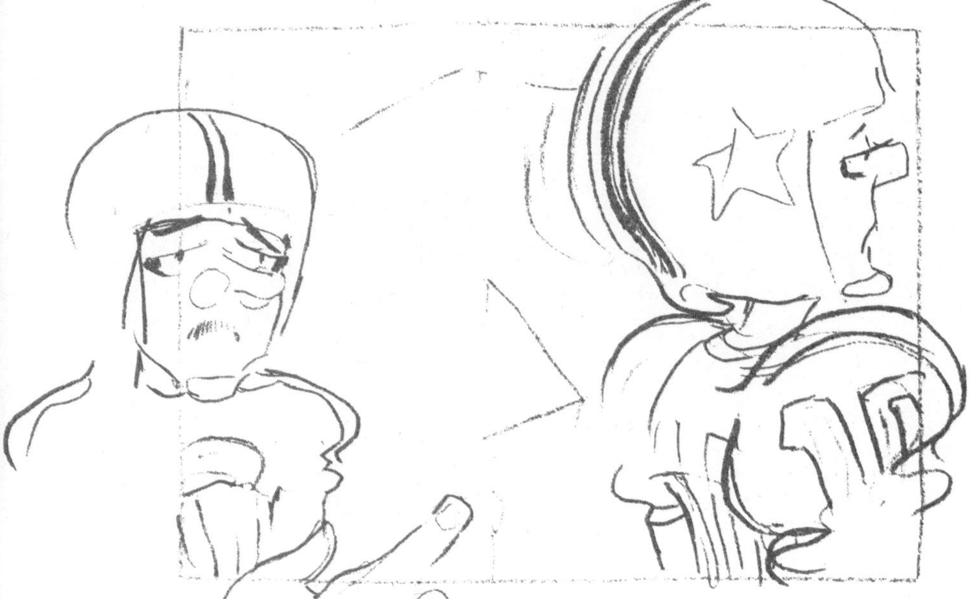

... WITH ALL, ...
KIRBY ENTERS AS B.D. EXITS –
TRACKING MOVEMENT ACCELERATES SLIGHTLY.
ZONKERS HAND APPEARS.

4

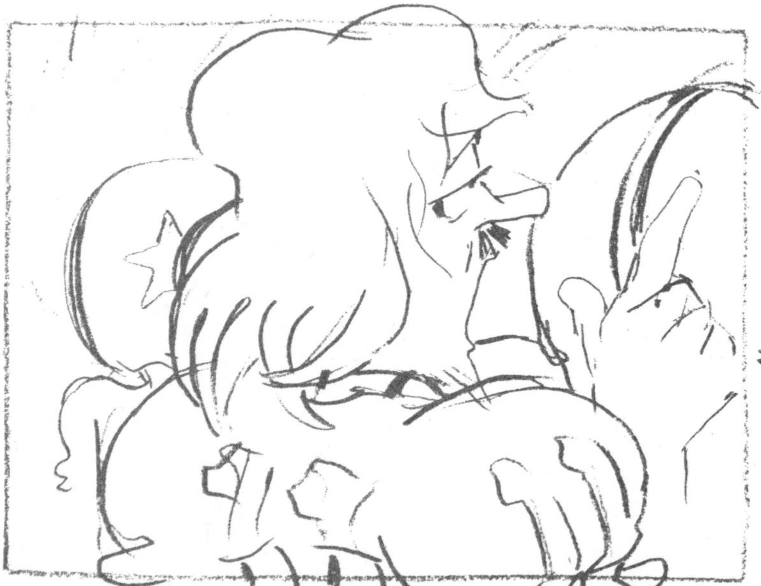
FWB·77

... HAS BECOME A GROTESQUE METAPHOR
CAMERA NOW CLEARLY ROTATING TO
LOOK DOWN HALLWAY – ZONKER REMAINS
IN CENTER OF FRAME ALTHOUGH HE IS
WALKING.

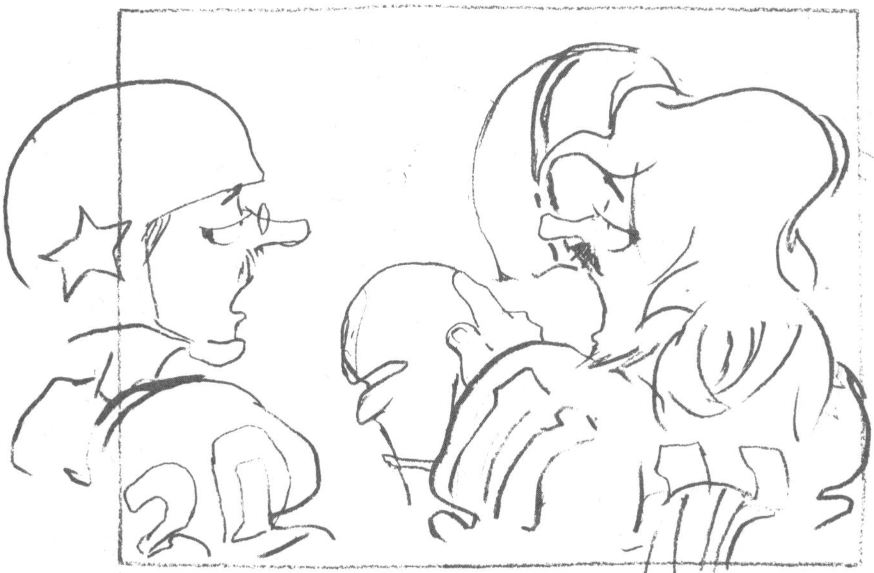

... FOR AMERICAN AGGRESSION IN INDOCHINA ...

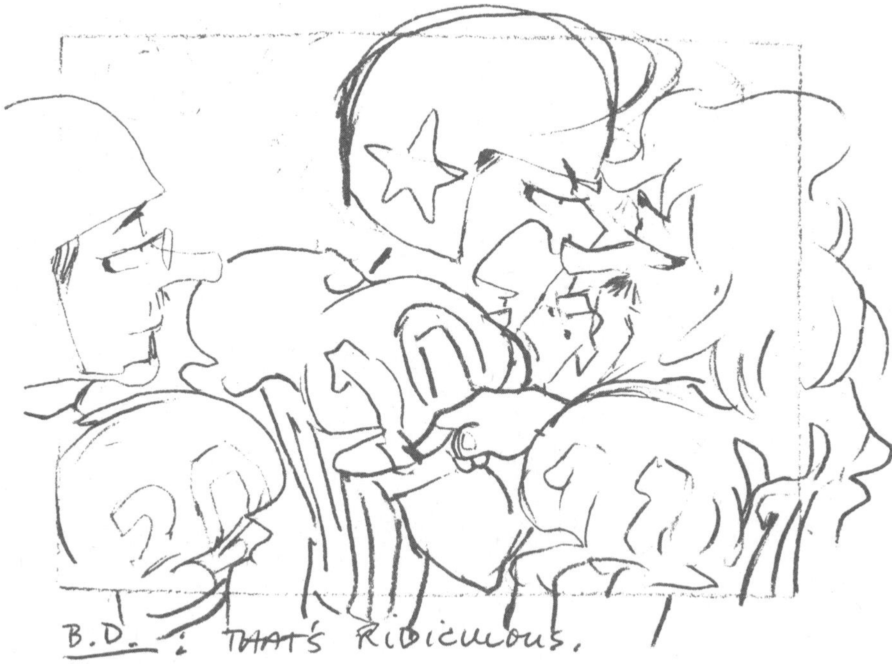

B.D.: THAT'S RIDICULOUS.

ZONKER

Well, not in any formal sense, Kirby. I mean, Americans played football
in the late twenties, and they were isolationists then...

KIRBY

Oh, so you think it's something subtler, something attitudinal...
*The three have reached the end of the tunnel. They walk over to the
benches.*

ZONKER

Exactly. The sport has lost its original graciousness. The comradely pitting
of skills is on the decline. Maiming is on the rise.

B.D.

Walking past them onto field where huddle is waiting
Tell you what, you two fellows can work it all out here on the
bench....We'll see you at halftime.

ZONKER
Still to Kirby

Don't get me wrong now, I'm all for sports. I still admire the thrill-of-
victory—agony-of-defeat dichotomy...
Voice trails off as we follow B.D. to his huddle.

B.D.

Hey, guys...

HUDDLE

Hey, Cap'n!

B.D.

Looking over at opposing lineup
Okay, what have we got here?

CAL

Bad news, man. That big dude Kawolsky's back. He got paroled.

B.D.

Damn! That makes them tough on the left. Okay, we'll go with a rollout to
Cal on the right. The rest of you chumps get out there and hit. And I want
Kawolsky taken out, understood? I don't care how you do it, but bury that
sucker. Kill him! Got it?!

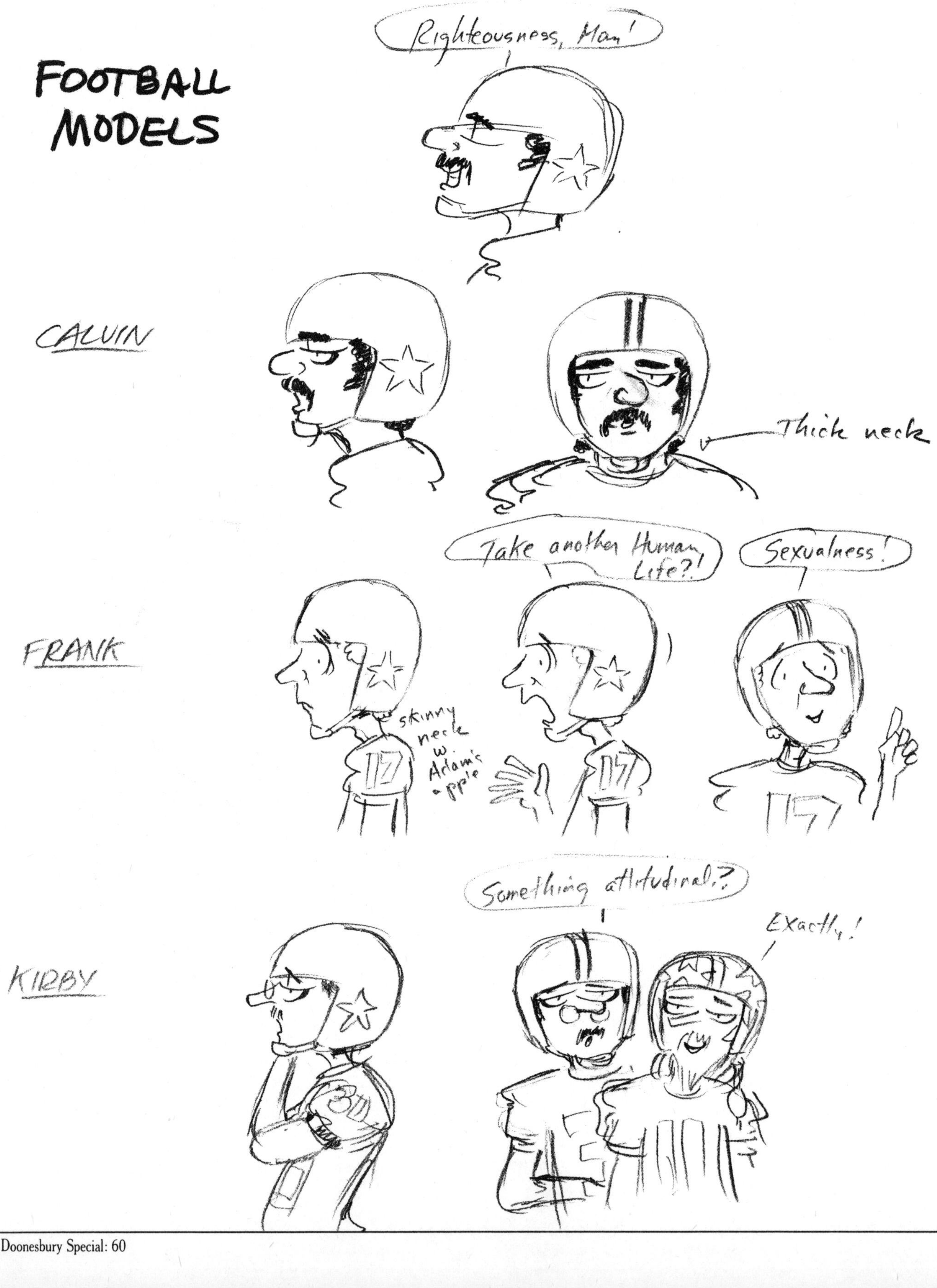
FOOTBALL MODELS
Righteousness, Man!
CALVIN
Thick neck
FRANK
Take another Human Life?!
Sexualness!
skinny neck w. Adam's apple
17
KIRBY
Something attitudinal?
Exactly!

Pen : Castell #2.5

Colors:
skin - Flesh #15
Shirt - grayed blue #10
Pants - Tan #14
Shoes - brown #19

helmet
eyes   } white
teeth

stripes
star   } yellow green #20

Notes:

1) eyes self lined white

2) black stripes on either side
   of green helmet stripe may
   need thickening in inking

HUDDLE
Aw right! Aw right!
Snort! Snort!

FRANK
B.D.?

B.D.
Later, Frank! On three, got it?

FRANK
B.D., listen, please! This can't wait! I'm a C.O.!

B.D.
What, Frank?

FRANK
A C.O. A conscientious objector! I can't kill anybody! Take another life?
A human life? And Kawolsky's? I know Kawolsky! We grew up to-
gether! In Queens, for god's sake! And you're asking me…

B.D.
Frank, Frank, listen to me, Frank. "Kill" is just a football term, Frank.
It's…uh…

CALVIN
Hyperbole, sir.

B.D.
Right, hyperbole. We're not really gonna kill Kawolsky! We just…

REFEREE
Delay of game! Five yards!

B.D.
Five ya—! Okay, Frank! Out of the game!

FRANK
But…

B.D.
Out! Now! Substitute!

Exit Frank. B.D. reforms huddle, Zonker's star-studded helmet suddenly appears.

B.D.
What the hell is this? Elton John?

ZONKER
Harris, sir. I've had a change of heart and mind. I'm ready to play ball, sir.

B.D.
Wonderful. All right now, have you all got it? We're going with a rollout to…Hey, Harris! What the hell are you smoking?

ZONKER
Maintain, Cap'n. Maintain. It's a perfectly harmless blend of seventeen herbs and spices found only in nature.

B.D.
I don't believe this! Are you crazy?!! Do you want us to get thrown out of the conference?

CALVIN
Putting a comradely arm around Zonker
Hey, Zonker, bad scene, man. Did you know a recent study at Tulane linked heavy usage with…

ZONKER
Nagging backache. Yeah…yeah, I heard.

CALVIN
No, man—brain damage! Dig this: Rhesus monkeys were given controlled daily dosages…
Players start to turn into monkeys
After only two weeks, intensive interviews were conducted with each of them…
Monkeys start interviewing one another

ZONKER
Don't tell me…

CALVIN
Right. They were all totally incoherent.

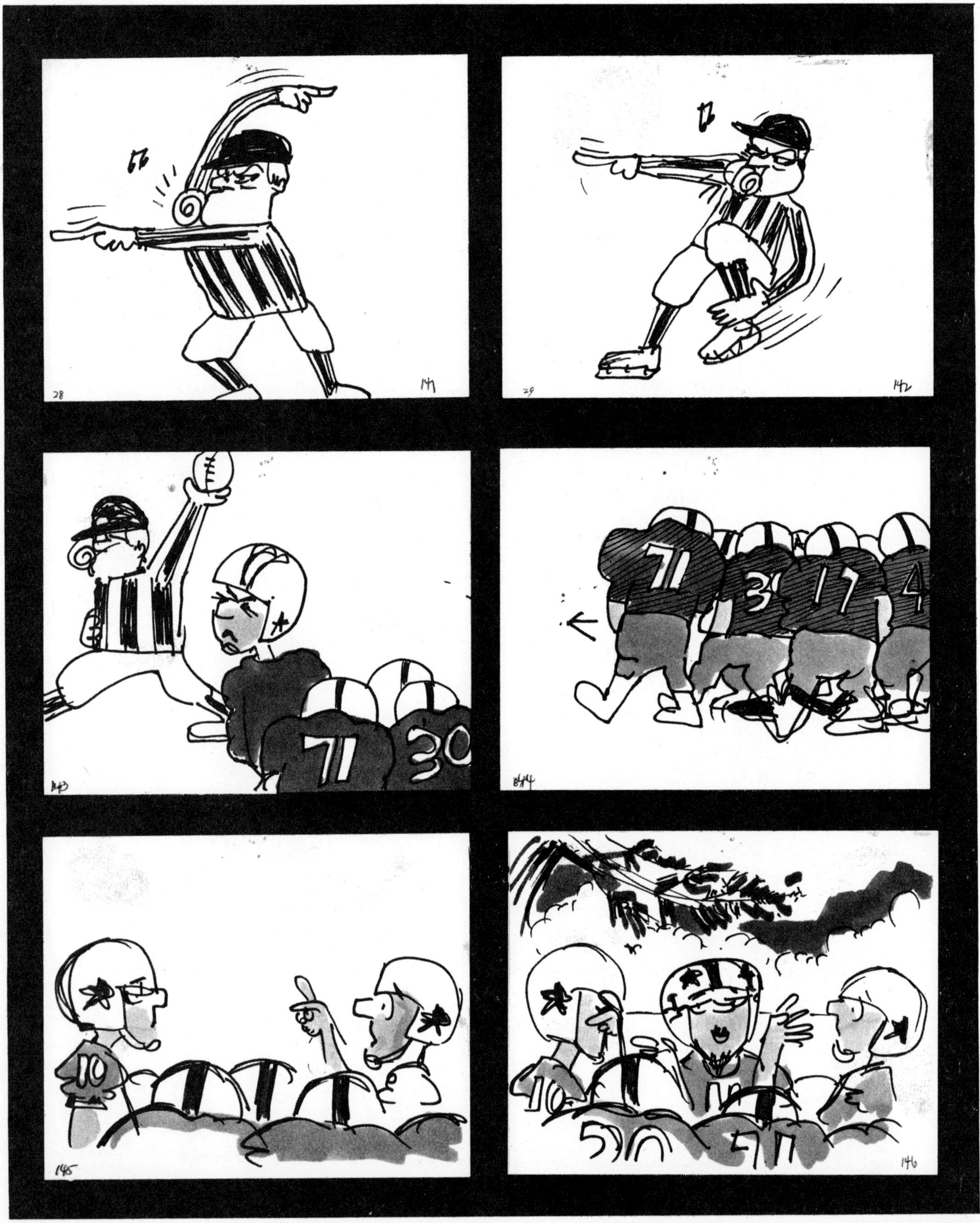

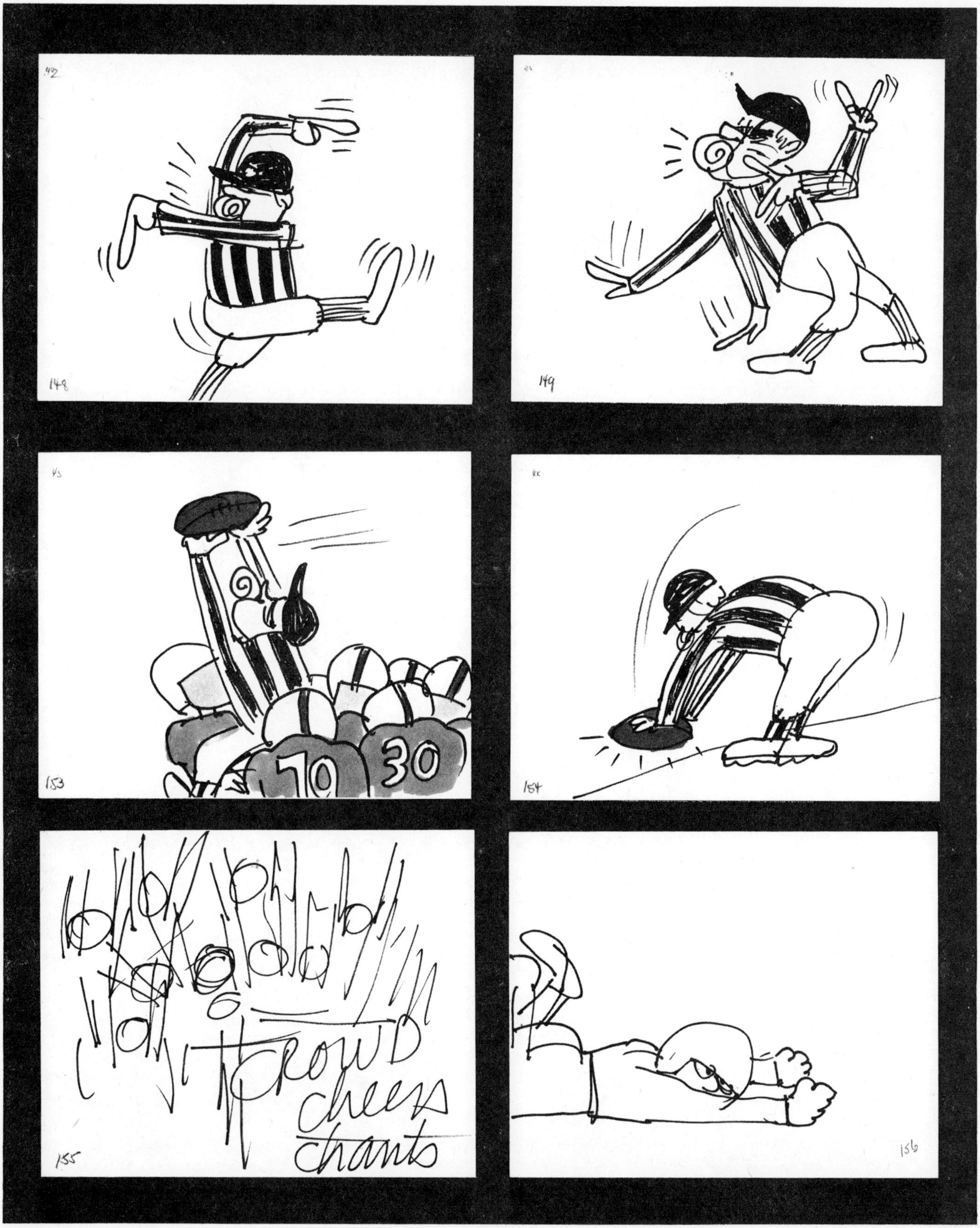
CROWD cheers chants

Colors: Pants - Gol. yellow #20

Helmet
Eyes
numbers } white

Stars
Stripes } yel. green #20

Skin - Flesh #15

Calvins Skin - Sun Flesh #17

Shirts - greyed Blue #10

Note:

1) eyes self lined white

2) two black stripes on either side of green helmet stripe often need thickening

3) Watch white highlights on shirt cuffs

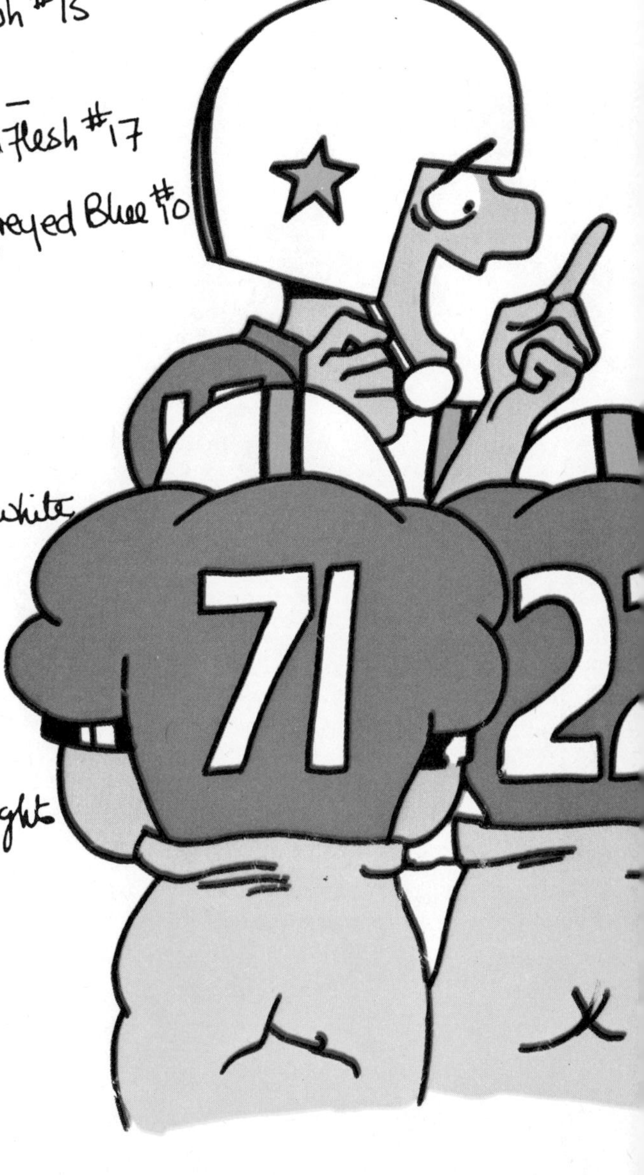
71

SHOES R.BR.19

INSIDE MOUTH M.R. 9

TONGUES VER.9

KIRBY'S HAIR BR.13

RALPH. " X-0.4.17

FRANK. " 0.4.20

KIRBY'S GLASSES – W

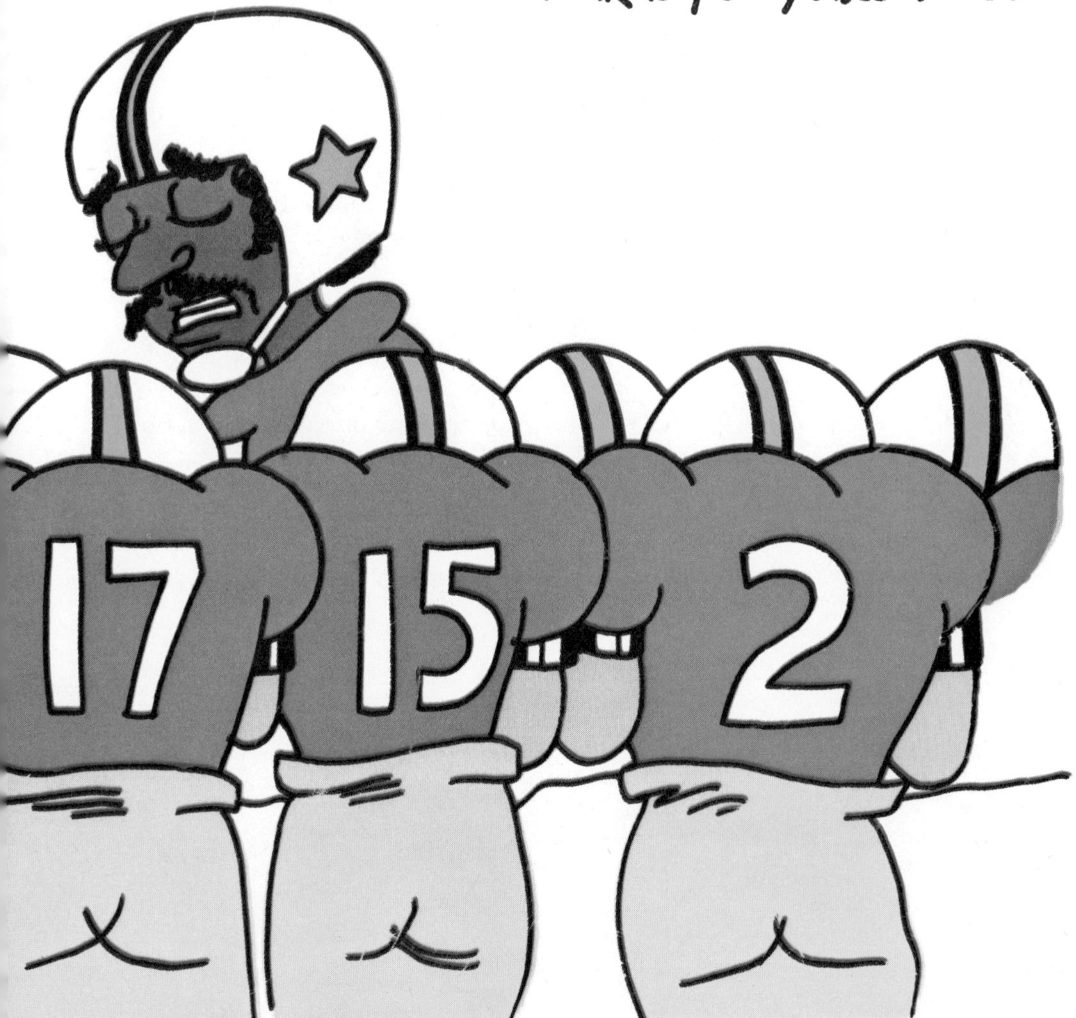

Monkeys turn back into players

ZONKER
Looking at joint
Oh, my god…

B.D.
Got the message, Superfly? And remember, Harris, you're on the team!
You're affecting the whole…

RALPHIE
Too late! I find myself about to succumb!

CALVIN
Me, too, man! I can't take the peer pressure any longer!

REFEREE
Delay of game! Five yards!

B.D.
That does it!
To huddle
Get back there!
Follows after
See that? See that? We're in the shadow of our own goal post!
Assumes control
Now, listen! It's a pass to Kirby! On four! Now go!

RALPHIE
Um…B.D.…What about a question-and-answer period?

B.D.
Question-and-answer period?!? Are you out of…

ZONKER
What is it, Ralphie? What's wrong?

RALPHIE
Well, it's kind of…philosophical…

ZONKER
Go with it. Go with the flow…

RALPHIE

Okay…I just want to know…well…where do old football players go to die?

B.D.

Oh, my god…

ZONKER

Good question, Ralphie. As I understand it, old football players go to Green Bay, Wisconsin, where, on the shores of Lake Michigan, beneath whispering pines and the open sky, they lie down and quietly, almost gratefully, expire.

RALPHIE

That's beautiful…

B.D.

That's ridiculous!

REFEREE

Delay of game! Five yards!

B.D.

AAAIIIEEEEE……

ZONKER

Look, if you can't be pleasant, why don't you just go take a shower?
Players start retreating into end zone. B.D. tears after them.

B.D.

Pause, while huddle reforms; begins to speak in deceptively calm voice
Five more yards and we'll be in the end zone. That's called a touchback.
That's two points for the other team.
Pause
Do you know how ticked off that will make me?!

ZONKER

That's it, let it flow. Let it all come out. Anger is a valid emotion.

RALPHIE

Happiness! My favorite emotion is happiness!

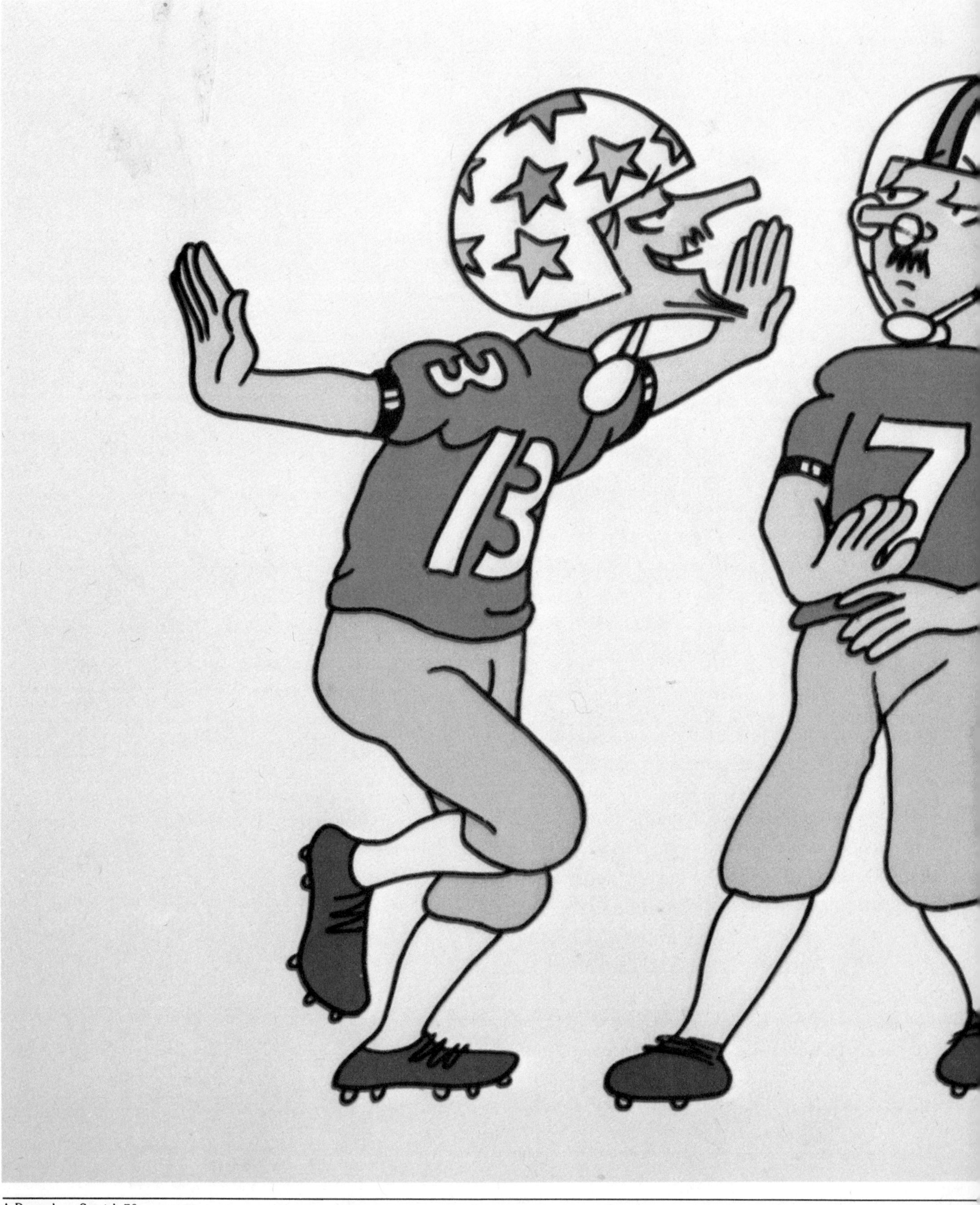

KIRBY

Or despair. Despair's a very top-drawer emotion.

CALVIN

So's righteousness, man!

ZONKER

And hunger!

RALPHIE

Hunger?

FRANK

Horniness!

EVERYBODY

Yeah, yeah, horniness.

B.D.

Horniness is not a valid emotion, dummy!

REFEREE

Delay of game! Touchback!

B.D.

AIIEEE!!!! I can't stand it! I can't stand it!

B.D. falls to his knees and starts pummeling the ground in a fit of impotent rage. Everybody else starts walking off the field until Zonker calls them back to look at B.D.

ZONKER

Catharsis, everybody, catharsis!

EVERYBODY

Where? Where catharsis?

KIRBY

Looking down at B.D.

Man, talk about valid emotions.

RALPHIE

Sure he didn't just hit his funny bone?

ZONKER
To Kirby

There you have it, Kirby. That's what losing does in this country. Paralysis of the spirit. See, Americans just don't understand the nobility of failure, you know, the way the Japanese do...

KIRBY
Yeah, but they like it.
Both are walking off field now

ZONKER
Still, all in all, Kirby, life can't always be first and goal to go...
Voice trails off as sound level of cheering crowd increases. Zoom slowly in on crowd, as cheering turns into crowd singing chorus of Jimmy's song. Singing fades. End of record is heard as we cut to Mike's hand removing arm from record on turntable. Pull back to see a contemplative Mike still sitting in Walden common room.

Back in living room, through door, we see B.D. watching TV; roaring of football crowd.

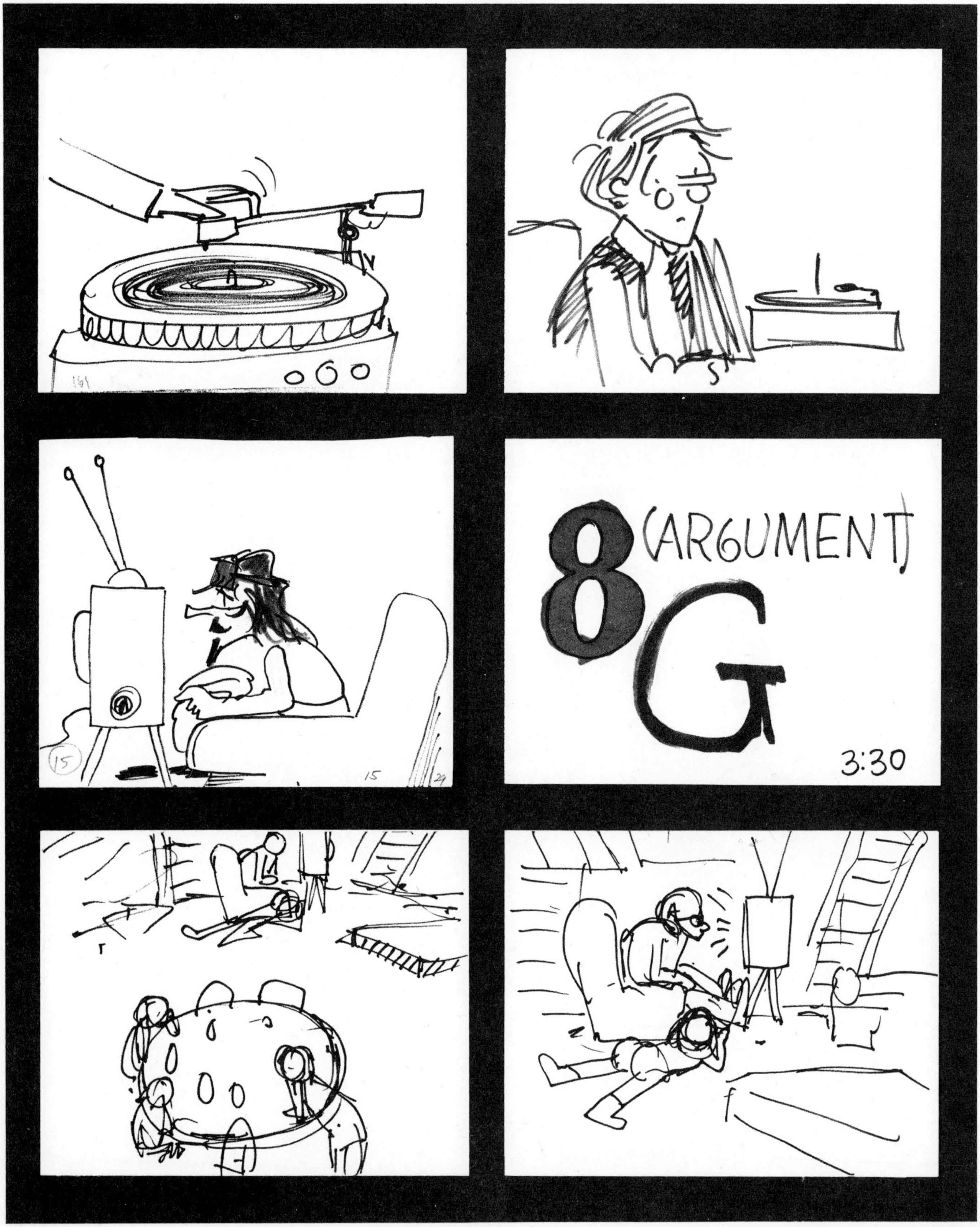

8 (ARGUMENT)
G
3:30

GIFFORD

MacAfee is down! Howard, he was hit very hard.

COSELL

You'll get no quarrel from me there, Gif. In fact, the doctors are rushing out onto the field, to ascertain whether this very gifted young athlete out of Tennessee State has been injured. And such must be the case, as young MacAfee, with whom I had breakfast this morning, is being put on a stretcher.

KARRAS

Howard, a sad note here: We just got word from our man on the field. It seems MacAfee is…uh…dead.
Roar of crowd turns into applause.

COSELL

Yes, but what a hand he's getting here, Alex!

KARRAS

Right! I'll tell you, Howard, these are some kind of football fans!
Roar of crowd continues. Pan back to living room.

B.D.

Turning off television
Dammit!
Pause. Boopsie looks up at him concerned
Geez, Boopsie, MacAfee was the only guy holding that ball club together.

BOOPSIE

I'm sorry, B.D.

B.D.

Walking into living room, Boopsie behind
If he'd just kept his head up! What an idiot!

MARK

In middle of conversation with Mike
Mike, all I'm saying…all I'm saying is we can't allow this to happen to ourselves. It's just as important as it always was to stand up and say we are responsible for what happens!

Mark:
  Skin. flesh #15
  hair. wood gray #20
  Pants. gray #18
  Sweater: X-vermillion #14
  shoes: gray #32

Beer can:

MIKE

Mark, we've been doing that for years. Hell, you and I have been civilly disobedient together as far back as I can remember…

MARK

But, where did it get us? What's it come to? Have we in any way prevented future Vietnams?

B.D.

Joining in

Future Vietnams? What the hell was wrong with the old one? We did what we had to over there!

MARK

We sure did. And we did it to 2.3 million children, 1.6 million…

B.D.

Yeah, yeah, I know the stats!…But it would have been worth it lasting-peace-wise if it hadn't been for that damn Prairie Populist with his…

BOOPSIE

Mr. McGovern? B.D., he and Lieutenant Shriver were decent men! Gosh, if they hadn't pricked our national conscience…

B.D.

We woulda won! Look, I know, baby, I was there. And I went there…

MIKE

…to get out of a term paper…

B.D

Wrong, Wimp-face, I joined because…

MIKE

I remember distinctly! You got a dean's excuse…

B.D.

Voice rising in genuine anger

Look, Doonesbury, if people like me hadn't gone it would have been domino-city for the gooks!

MARK

You hear that? You hear that? This, friends, is why we came within an eyelash of intervention in Angola!

B.D.

Which we punted! Completely! And to a bunch of skinny, tequila-crazed Marxist Cubans!

MIKE

To Boopsie

Why isn't he watching the game?

B.D.

That's a damn good example! You let those swarthy little maniacs loose, and they'll take over the world!

BOOPSIE

His favorite halfback was killed.

B.D.

I mean, my god, look what they did to Miami!

MARK

Addressing the room

Ladies and Gentlemen, this is what I am talking about! The problem has not gone away! It belongs in the Smithsonian; but even as we speak, it lives and breathes and drinks beer right here in our own living room!

Joanie has entered living room. She walks between Mark and B.D. and picks up some glasses.

JOANIE

Walking back to kitchen

You know something, guys, I think you're all missing the point. You don't see how your pasts have affected you, how they've prevented you from growing. Zonker was right.

This is heavy stuff. B.D. and Mark are immobilized, but Mike follows her into kitchen and leans against door. Joanie goes back to washing dishes.

MIKE

You think so, Joanie?

JOANIE

Well, I think I know something of the necessity of change. I've felt rage
with the best of them.

MIKE

You mean, your old man back in Denver?

JOANIE

Uh-huh. But I stopped fighting it. And him. My last batch of perfect
french fries was delivered to the dinner table on July 21, 1972.

MIKE

After pause
You still make the best.

JOANIE

Yeah, but not in Denver. That's a very important distinction. I've got so
much here…

MIKE

The day care…

JOANIE

Yeah, the day care. That's been the key, I think. That's when I learned
something of hope, and something of the pointlessness of despair. Mike,

JOANIE

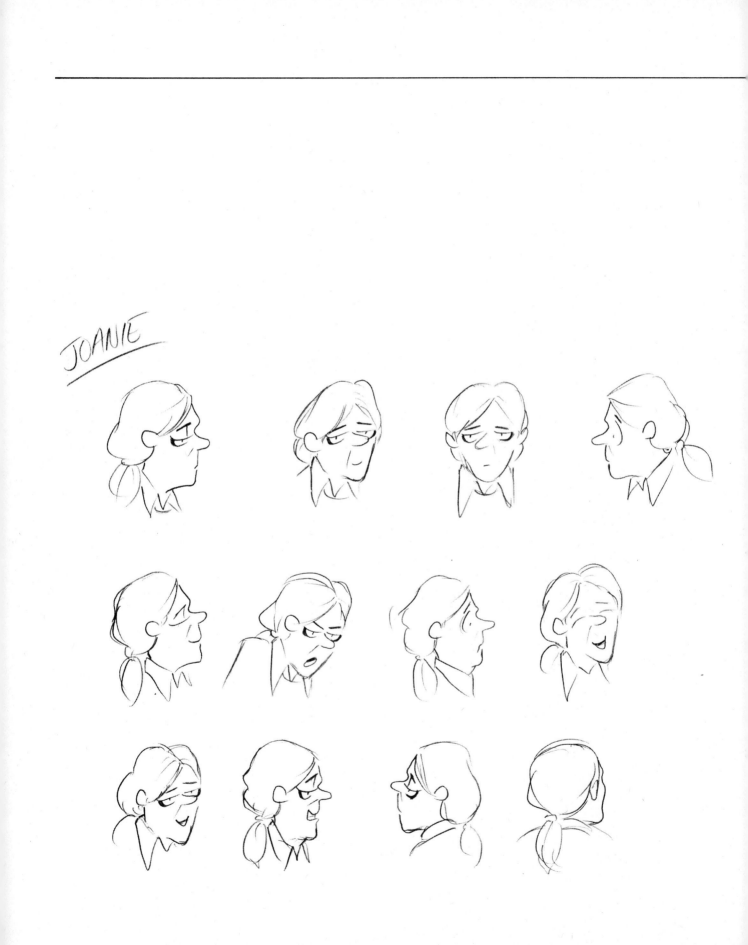

JOANIE as
Perfect Housewife

(The Mary/Hartman
look)

it's a whole new generation of hearts and minds out there, and that challenge goes a long way in justifying the earlier pain. I mean, in some respects, it isn't a whole lot different than just being a hassled mother. It's the same struggle to get through the day—taking care of kids,

Children's noise level rises

feeding them, supervising them, picking up after them, stopping their fights…

JOANIE
But I'm getting paid for it!
Pull back to reveal Joanie at day-care center

CATHY
How much?
Crash of building blocks in background

JEAN
Off camera
WAAH!

JOANIE
Not enough, honey.
Walks over to table covered with building blocks. Ellie and Jean are on the left with most of the blocks. Howie is at the other end hard at work with four or five blocks.

ELLIE
Jean!
Jean's crying
You're not trying! How're you ever going to be a building contractor if…

JEAN
Waaaah! I don't wanna be a building contractor!

ELLIE
Oh, Jean, now, you're being such a baby! Now c'mon, you've got an aptitude…Joanie told me…

JOANIE
Now, Ellie, I didn't exactly say that…I…

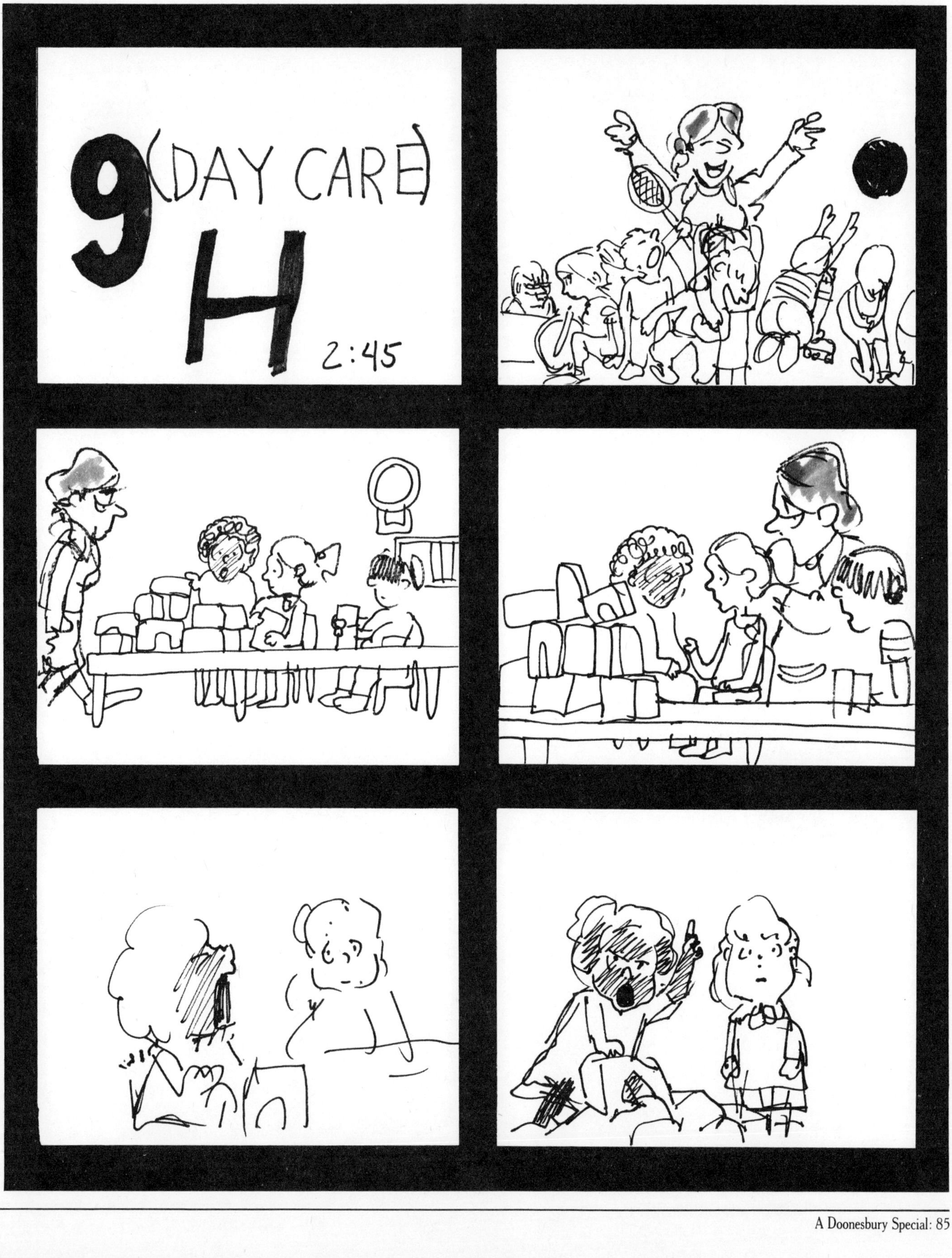
9 (DAY CARE)
H
2:45

 JEANIE

HOWIE

ELLIE

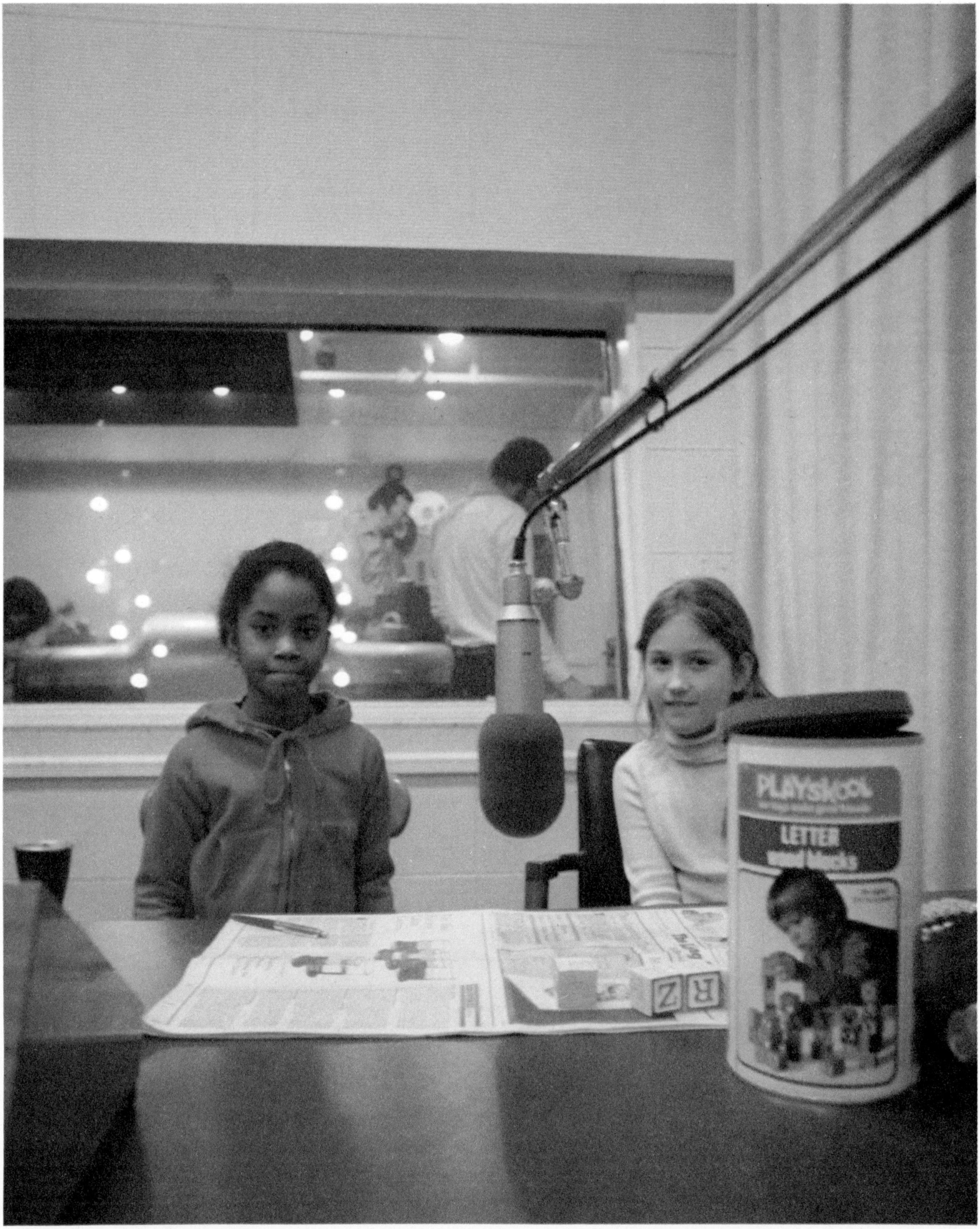
PLAYSKOOL
LETTER

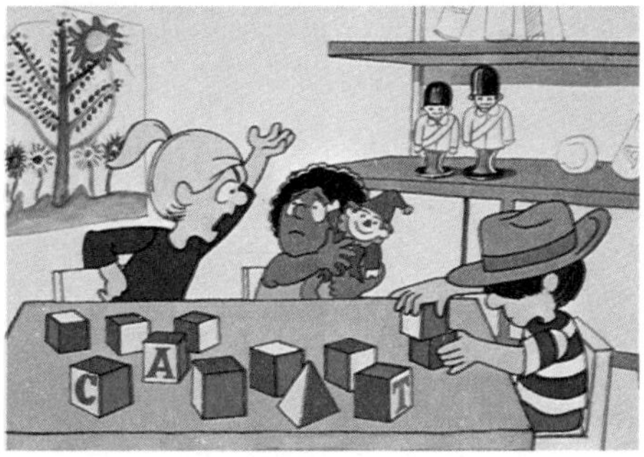

ELLIE
Critically
Joanie, I'm trying to build up her confidence...

JEAN
I don't wanna be a building contractor!

ELLIE
Well, then, what are you going to do with your life, huh? Just fritter it away? What are you going to be?...

JEAN
A baby-sitter

ELLIE
To Joanie
You know what the problem is here, don't you?

JEAN
I'm good with kids, really.

ELLIE
Do you know why Jeanie won't build? Do you know?

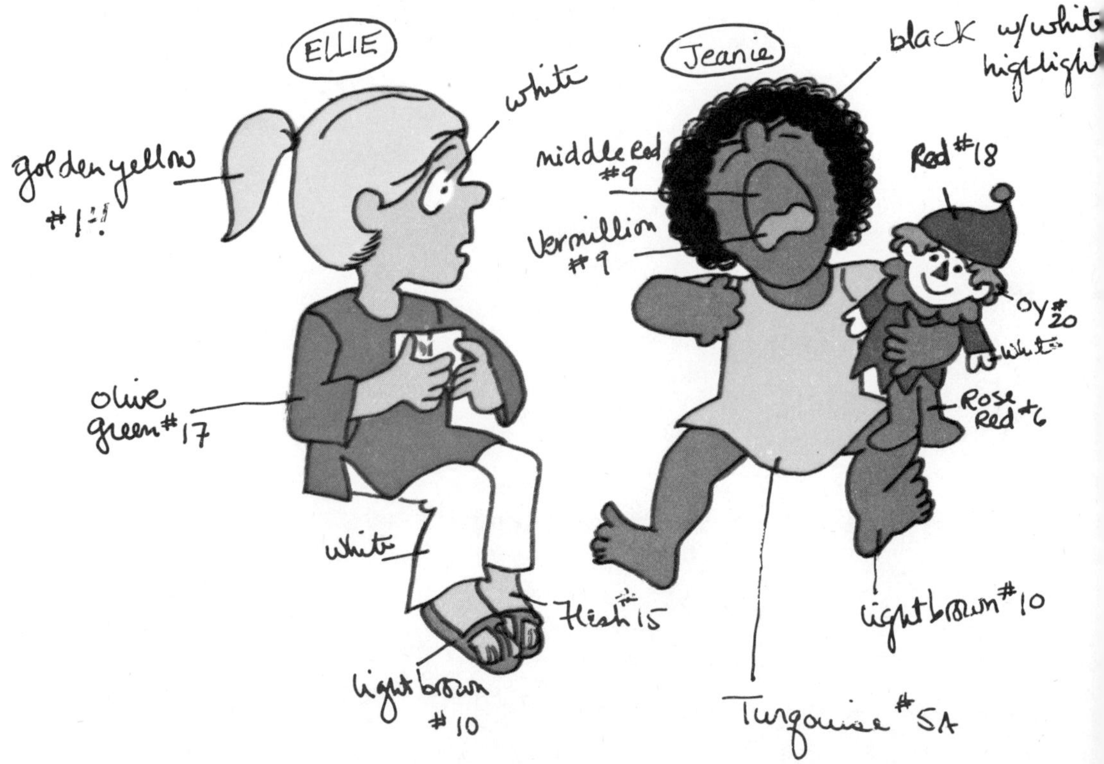

ELLIE
Jeanie
black w/white highlight
white
golden yellow
middle Red #9
Vermillion #9
Red #18
OY #20
white
Rose Red #6
olive green #17
white
Flesh #15
light brown #10
light brown #10
Turquoise #5A

HOWIE
Mock seriousness
Why won't Jeanie build?

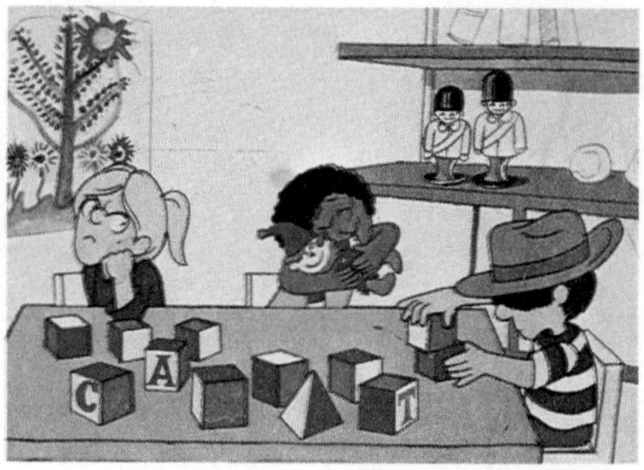
C
A
T

ELLIE
Jean won't build because there are no good role models in the construction industry. Especially for blacks.

JEAN
Ella Fitzgerald is black.

ELLIE
Ella Fitzgerald is not a building contractor!

JOANIE
Now, wait a minute. Ellie's raised a valid point here. Let's talk about people whose lives you respect. Who are your role models?

HOWIE
Abe Beame.
Building he has been working on collapses.

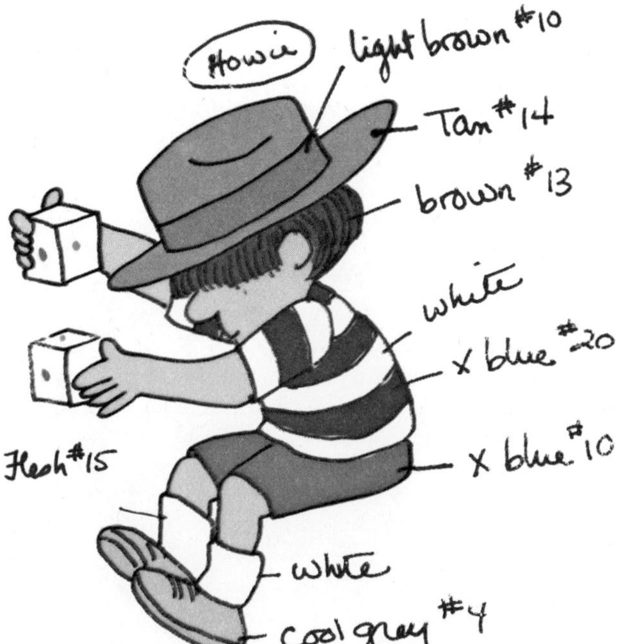
Howie
light brown #10
Tan #14
brown #13
white
x blue #20
Flesh #15
x blue #10
white
cool gray #4

Joanie

① ④

1. Flesh #15
White
woodgray #10
Orange #17
x·ov. #8

4. light brown #10
white
black
middle Red #9
Vermillion #9
grey #4
oy #20
grey #32

5. black
White
light brown #10
blue v. #9
Red #18
x oy #8

6. Flesh #15
White
brown #13
Rose Red #6
grey #7

7. Flesh #15
White
Redbrown #19
Red #18
middle Red #9

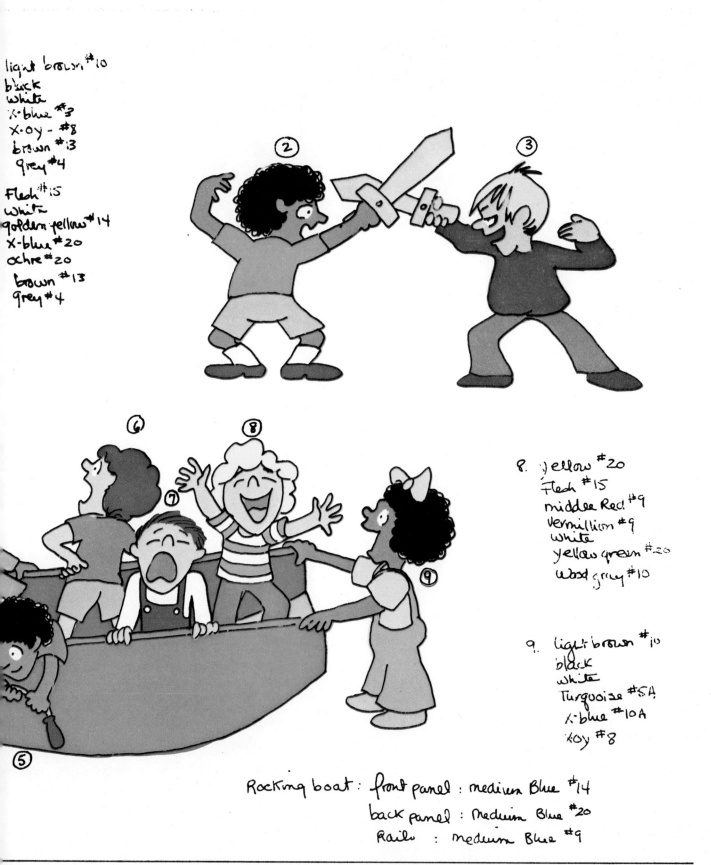

light brown #10
black
white
X-blue #3
X-oy - #8
brown #13
grey #4

Flesh #15
white
golden yellow #14
X-blue #20
ochre #20
brown #13
grey #4

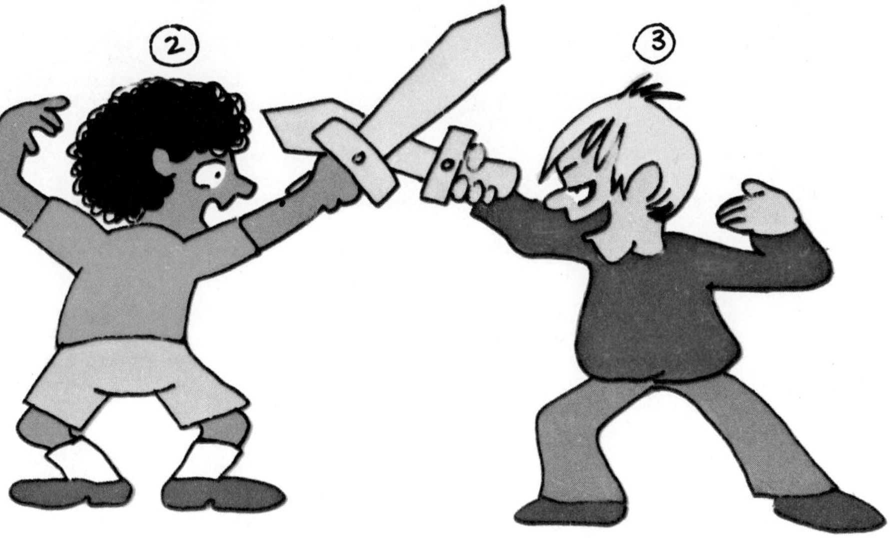
2
3

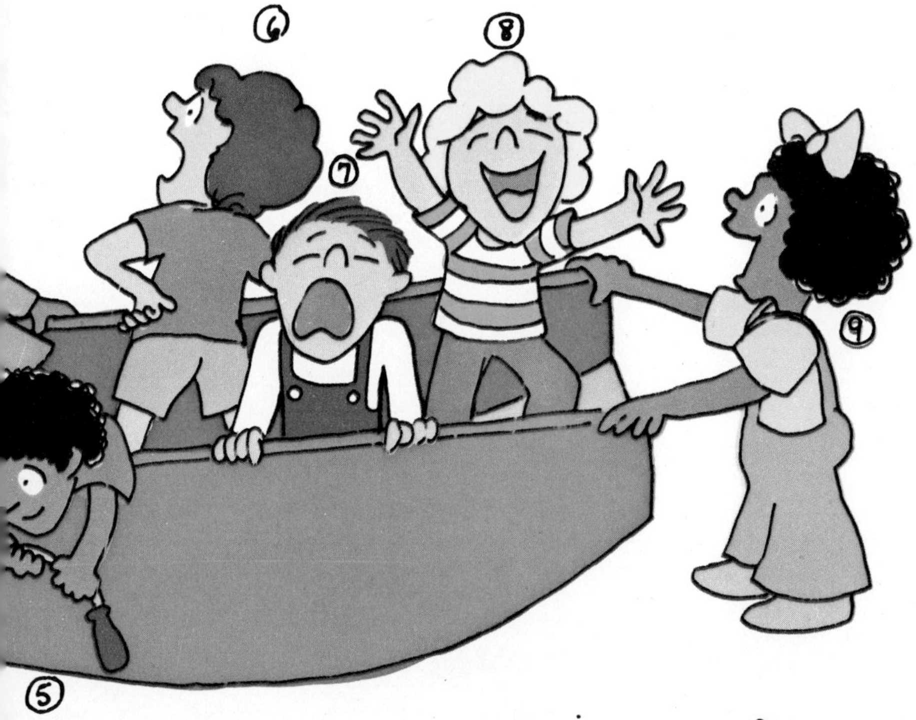
6
8
7
9
5

8. yellow #20
Flesh #15
middle Red #9
Vermillion #9
white
yellow green #20
Wood grey #10

9. light brown #10
black
white
Turquoise #5A
X-blue #10A
X-oy #8

Rocking boat: front panel : medium Blue #14
back panel : Medium Blue #20
Rails : medium Blue #9

ELLIE
Well, I used to think I'd like to be like Billie Jean King. But then I heard about how tennis makes one arm bigger than the other.

HOWIE
I meant Abe Beame, the accountant.

ELLIE
So after shopping around a bit, I switched from tennis to anthropology. I'm very into Margaret Mead now.

JOANIE
Margaret Mead?

ELLIE
Yes, I'd like to study sex in the Caribbean.

HOWIE
Perhaps I could keep the books.

JEANIE
To Joanie
Can I study sex in the Caribbean?

ELLIE
No, Jeanie, I already dibsied it. Besides, I'm telling you, your future's in high-rise single-dwelling ranch families.

HOWIE
In what?

ELLIE
C'mon, I'm going to show you how to build one…

JEAN
I don't wanna…

JOANIE
Go on, Jean, try it, just for me…

JEAN
Still sniffling
Well…

HOWIE
Without looking up
It'll never stand.

JEAN
Bristling at Howie's taunt
Oh, yeah?
Turns to blocks. Together Jeanie and Ellie proceed to build a small but perfect replica of the Chrysler Building. They step back to proudly examine their work.

JOANIE
Very nice, girls.
Howie's five-block structure at the end of the table collapses. Joanie looks back at Howie, who is obviously very badly shaken.

HOWIE
Ms. Caucus, may I be frank with you?

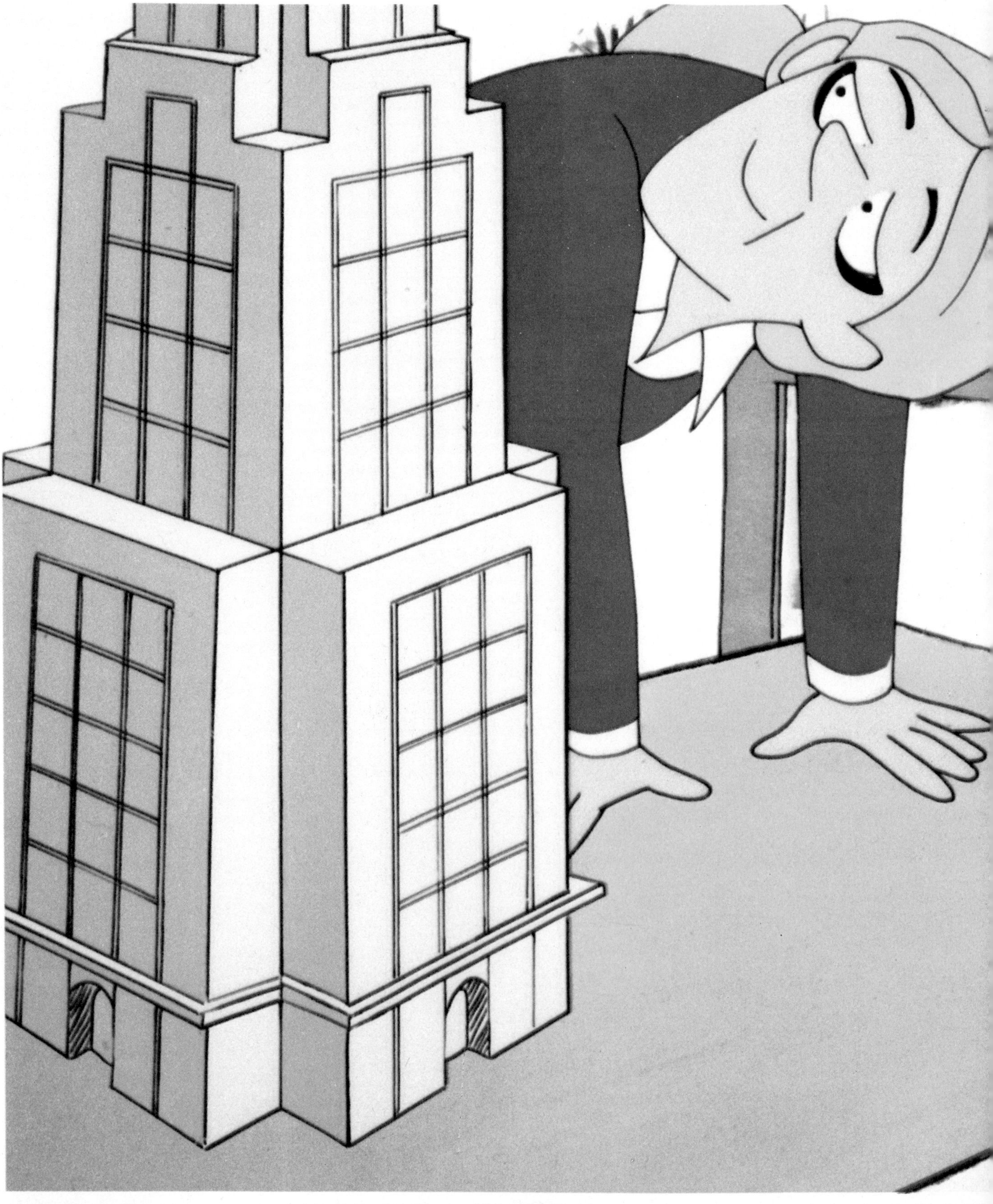

JOANIE

Sure, Howie, of course…

HOWIE

Ms. Caucus, ever since you got here, there's been a big change in the girls…

ELLIE

Correcting him

Women!

HOWIE

See? They keep acting like boys…

JOANIE

Well, Howie, I'm not sure you're being quite fair.…A great lady, Simone de Beauvoir, once said that there are two kinds of people: human beings and women. And when women start acting like human beings, they are accused of trying to be men.

HOWIE

Confused

Yeah…but…uh…

ELLIE

Simone de Beauvoir's got your number, Slim.

Phone rings.

JEAN

That's probably her now.

Joanie answers phone.

JOANIE

Walden Child Care. Oh, hi, Scot…Oh, no, I'm sorry, I forgot to ask the kids.…Hold on. Hey, everybody, Reverend Sloan needs some shepherds for his Christmas rock pageant. Any takers?

ELLIE

Is he taking affirmative-action cases?

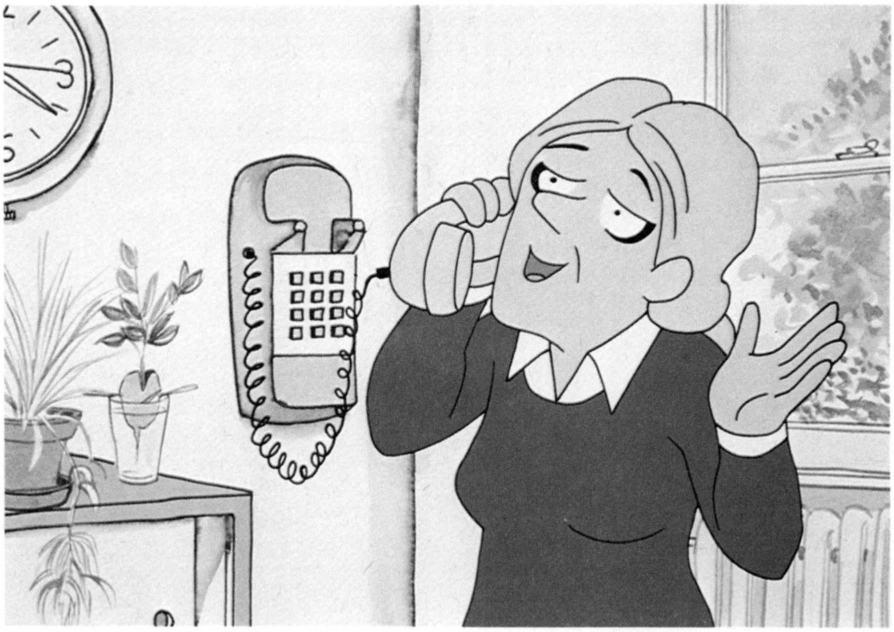

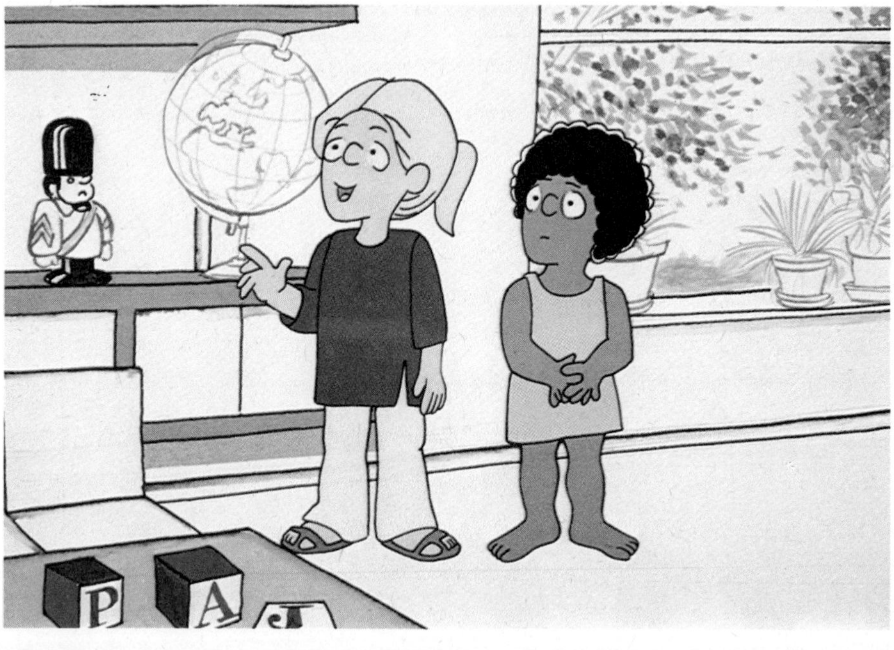
P
A

JOANIE
Into phone
Shepherdesses okay?
To Ellie
Yes.

ELLIE
Count me in.
Pan right. Ellie looks to Jeanie.

JEAN
Me, too. As long as the nude scenes are tasteful.

HOWIE
Resignation
Sigh.

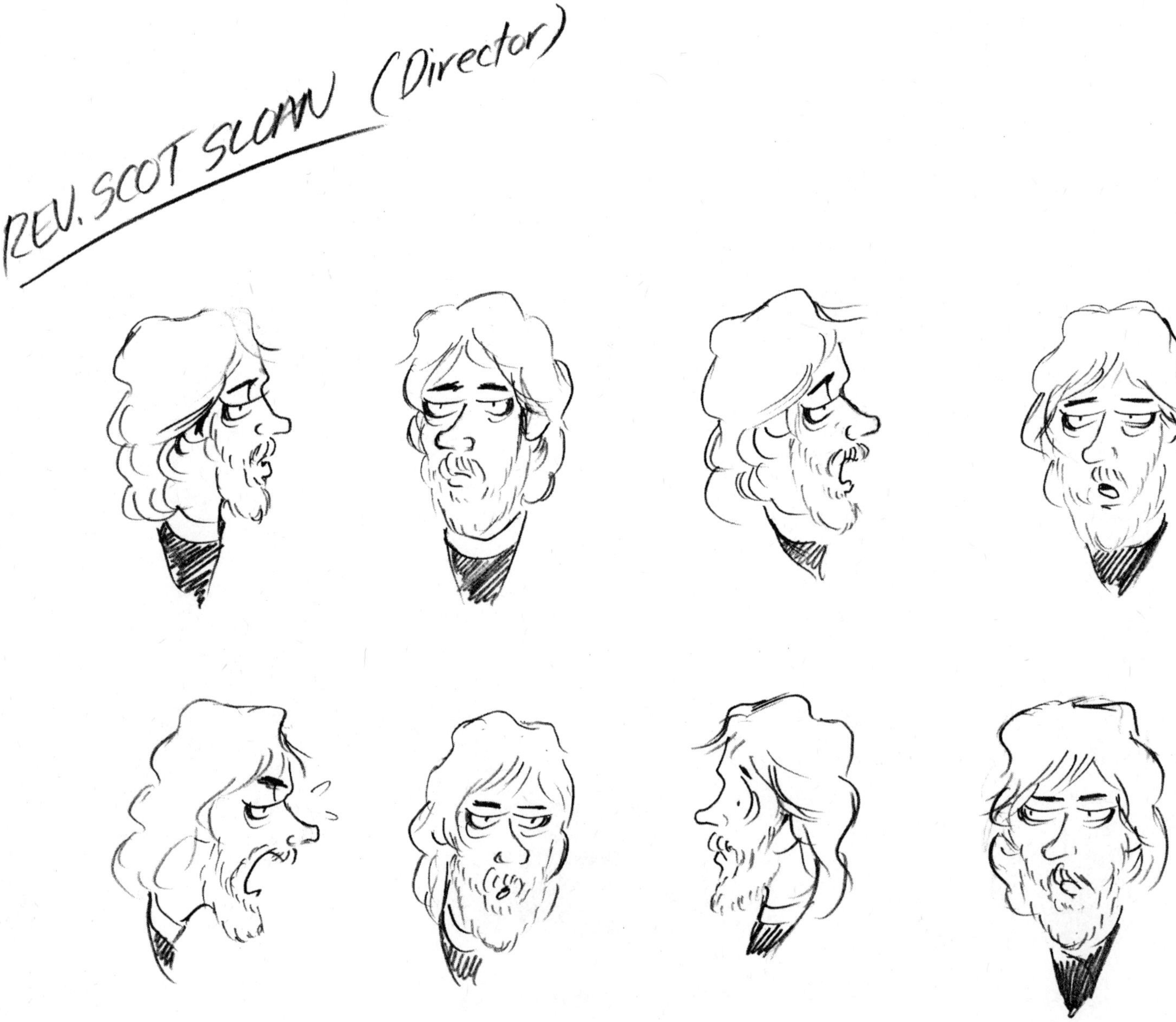
REV. SCOT SLOAN (Director)

In tight. Loud rock music begins.
Howie spins; as he comes around, pull back. All three are dressed up in shepherd costumes, doing Temptations steps.

SCOT
Off-camera
Spin, people, spin! This is the visitation!

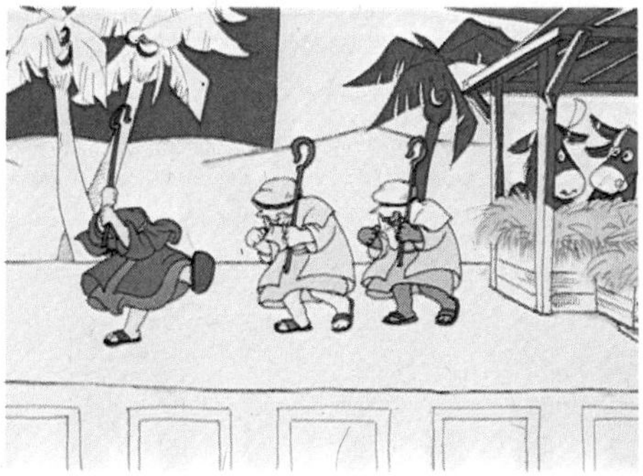

Ellie, Jean, and Howie are dancing on the Bethlehem set in a local school auditorium. Each has a mike and is doing soul-dance footwork. Ellie and Jean sing like angels and are perfectly coordinated in their moves. Howie is tripping over his microphone cord and obviously completely tone-deaf. They are singing "Come All Ye Faithful" with a rock beat.

SCOT
Off-camera
Good, good...uh, third shepherd, you're out of step....Better....Sing louder, third shepherd, Baby Jesus can't hear you!

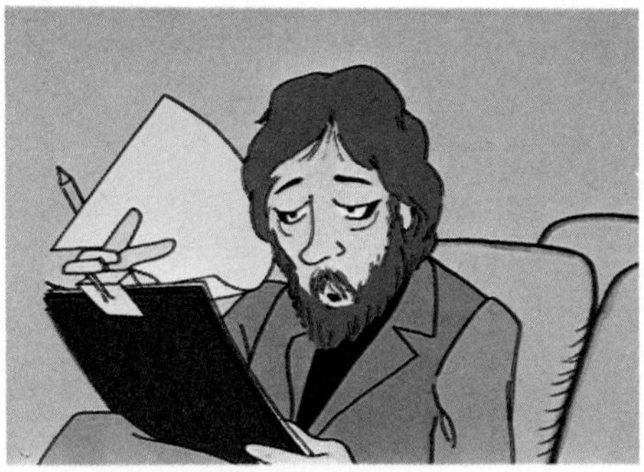

Howie trips again over microphone cord, and falls into manger. Joseph (Rufus), who has been playing rhythm guitar while a sheep flails away at a set of drums behind him, looks down at Howie, shakes his head, unplugs guitar, and walks down to first row of auditorium, where Scot is seated with clipboard.

RUFUS
Director?

SCOT
Not now, Rufus...

RUFUS
Director, I don't want to be Joseph anymore.

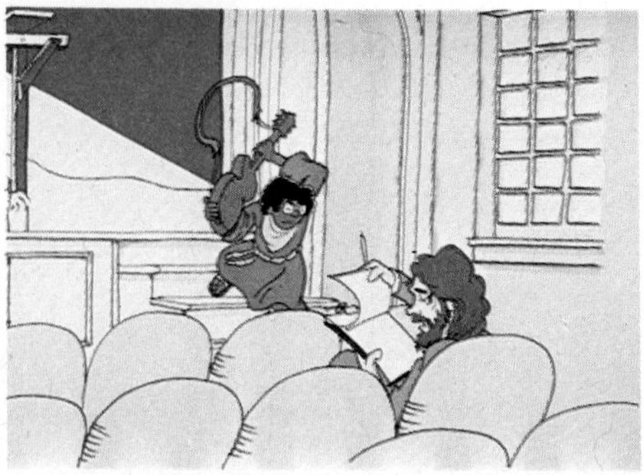

SCOT
Rufus, this is dress rehearsal. People are going to walk through that door any min—
Senses Rufus needs stroking
Rufus, Joseph is a major role! I had you in mind from the very beginning!

RUFUS

He's boring. Joseph is very boring. There is absolutely no character development.

SCOT

Rufus, that's just wrong. Joseph is a father figure. Strong, silent…

RUFUS

Look, why don't you just recast me as a Nubian slave?

SCOT

Horrified

In this day and age?

RUFUS

Okay, then, a Nubian waiter

SCOT

Losing patience

Get up there!

Rufus sighs but complies. Jean and Ellie get to the chorus of "Oh, Come…," and gesture in adulation at manger. Howie surfaces, straw in hair. Song ends with a burst of horrendous guitar playing as Joseph plugs in again. Exit Jean and Ellie.

VIRGIN MARY

In tentative voice

Well, Joseph, it's been quite a night…

SCOT

Off-camera

Louder!

VIRGIN MARY

Well, Joseph, it's been quite a night. That makes three shepherds and a magus.

RUFUS

Verily, Mary, and here cometh another!

Hits guitar chord. Pause as nothing happens.

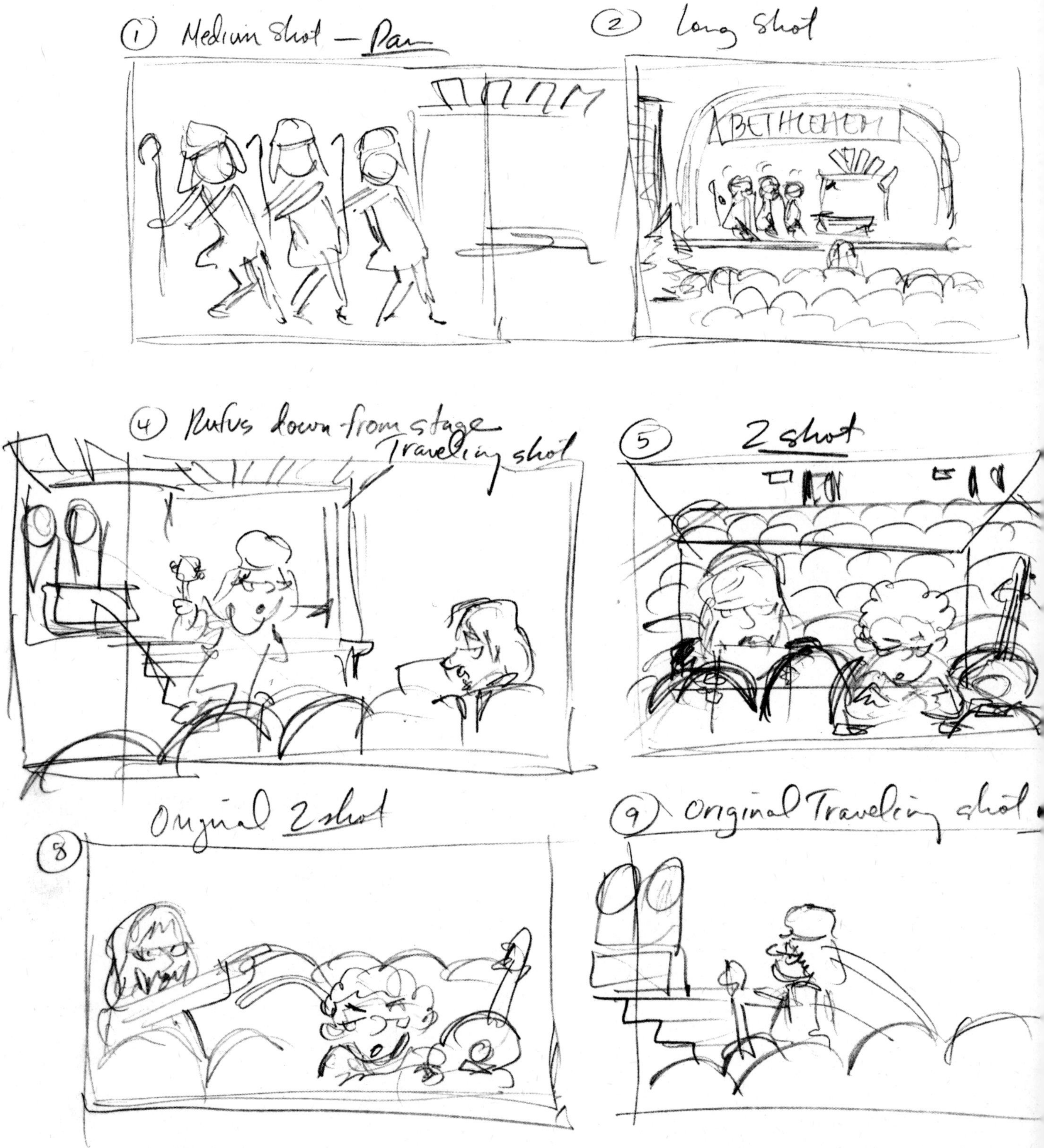
1 Medium shot — Pan
2 long shot
BETHLEHEM
4 Rufus down from stage Traveling shot
5 2 shot
Original 2 shot
8
9 Original Traveling shot

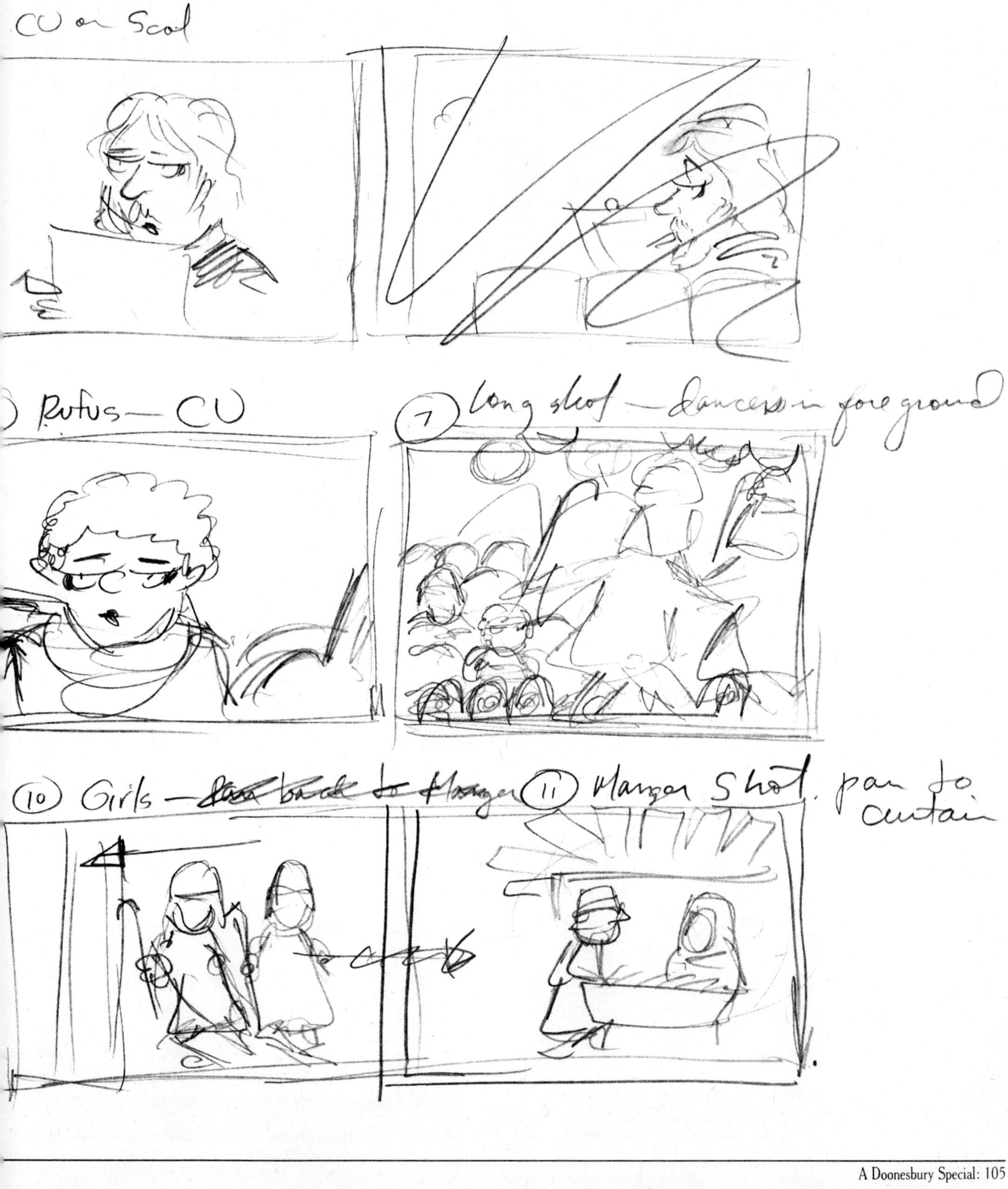

CU on Scot
Rufus — CU
7 Long shot — dancers in foreground
10 Girls — pan back to Manger
11 Manger Shot. pan to curtain.

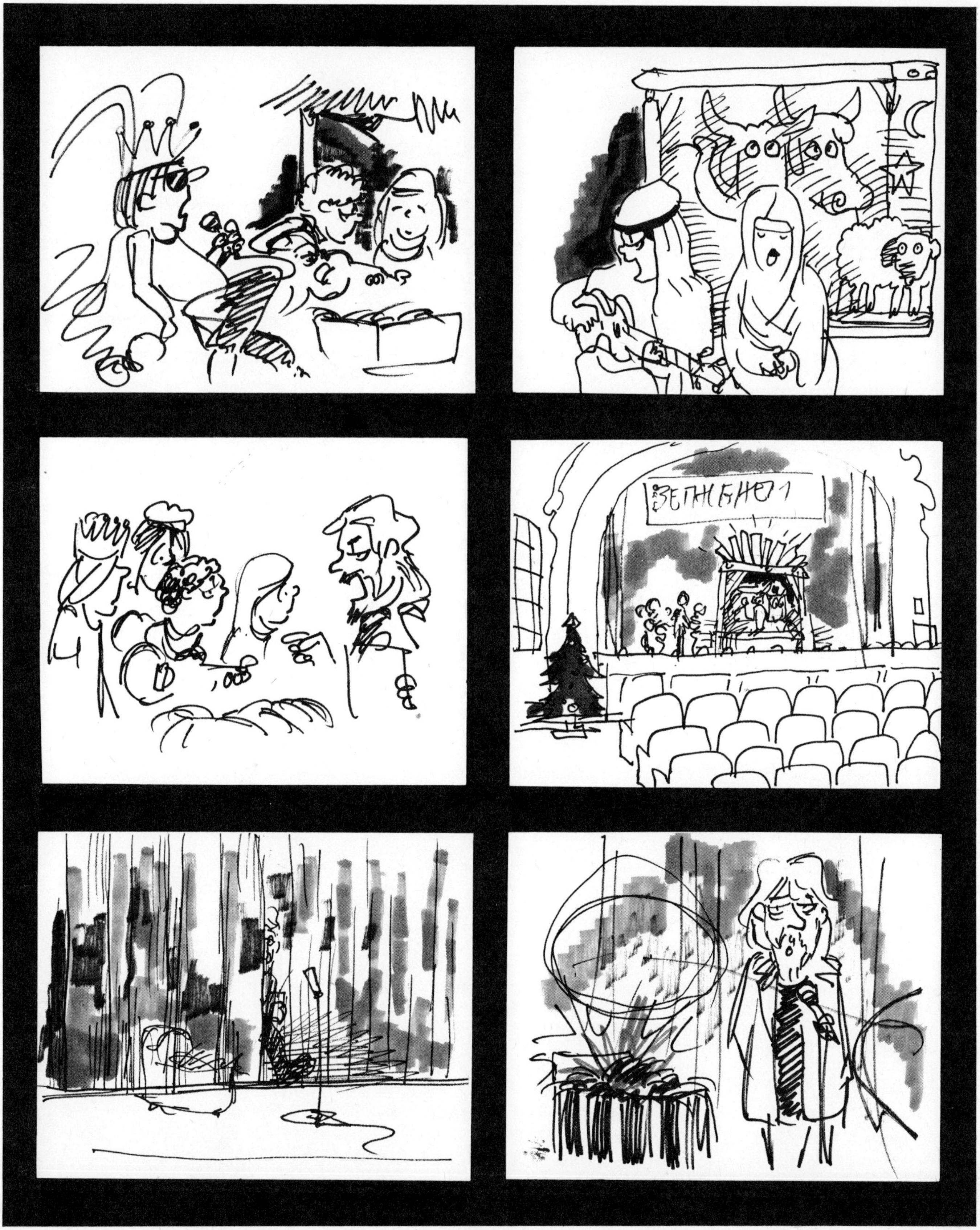

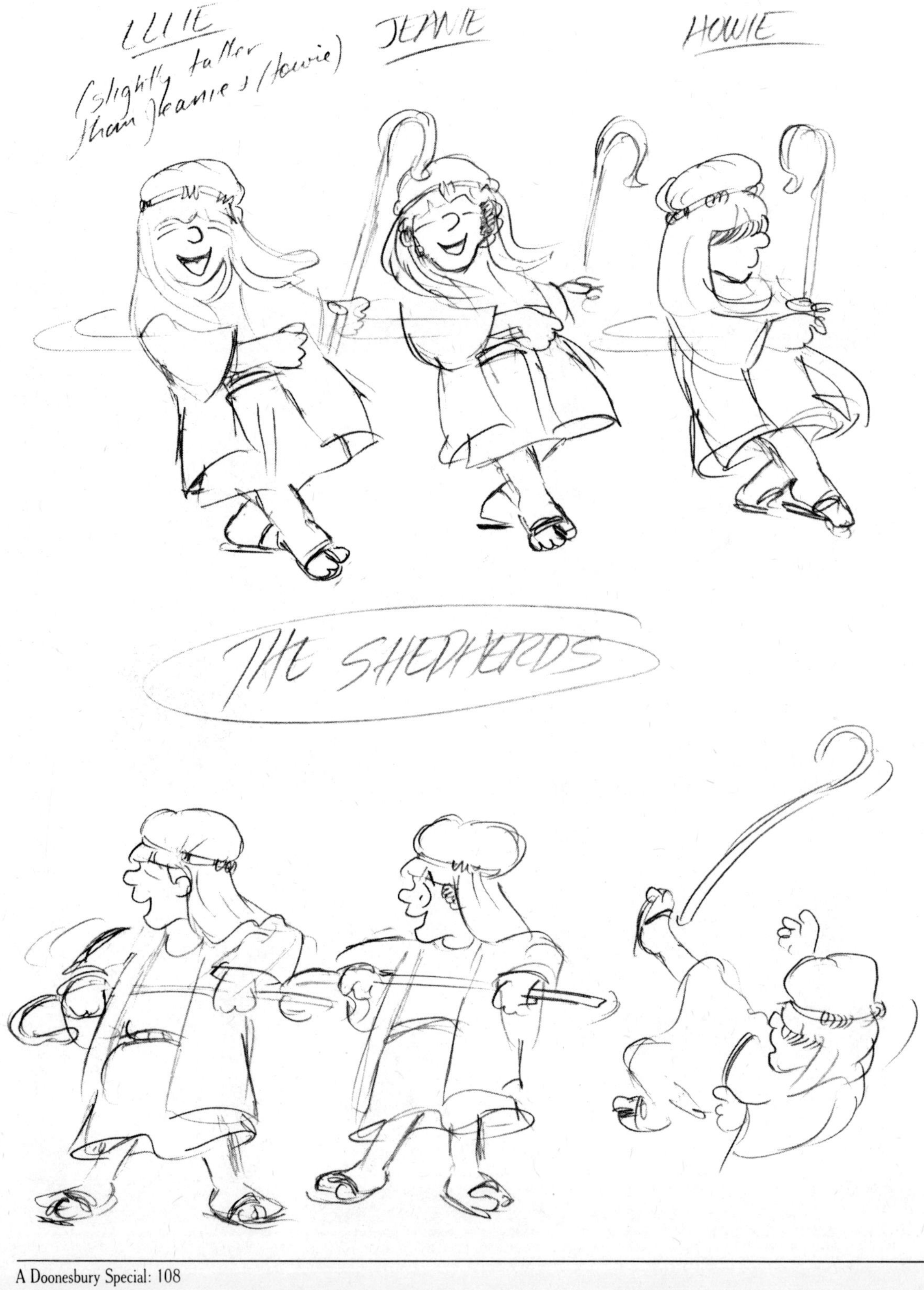
(slightly taller than Jeannie & Howie)
HOWIE
THE SHEPHERDS

HAIR —BLACK
(FLESH — SUN FL 17)
(GUITAR-BAND-EDGE)

GUITAR- OR-19
GUITAR PLATES COOL GR-4
   "   "   HI LITE " " 15
COLLAR
BELT   TAN 10
LEG STRAPS
SHOE SOLES COOL GR15
ROBE   OL-GRN 17

2 STRINGS

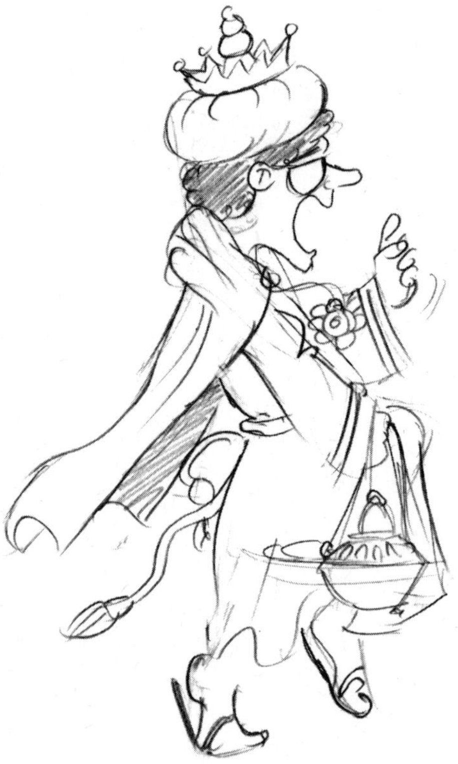

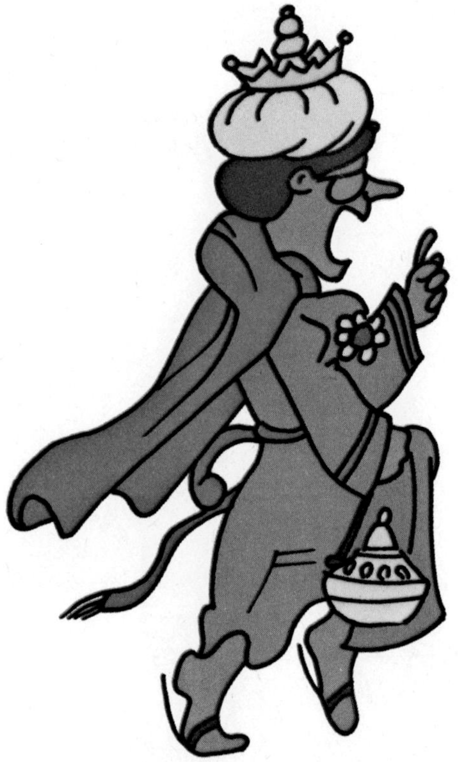

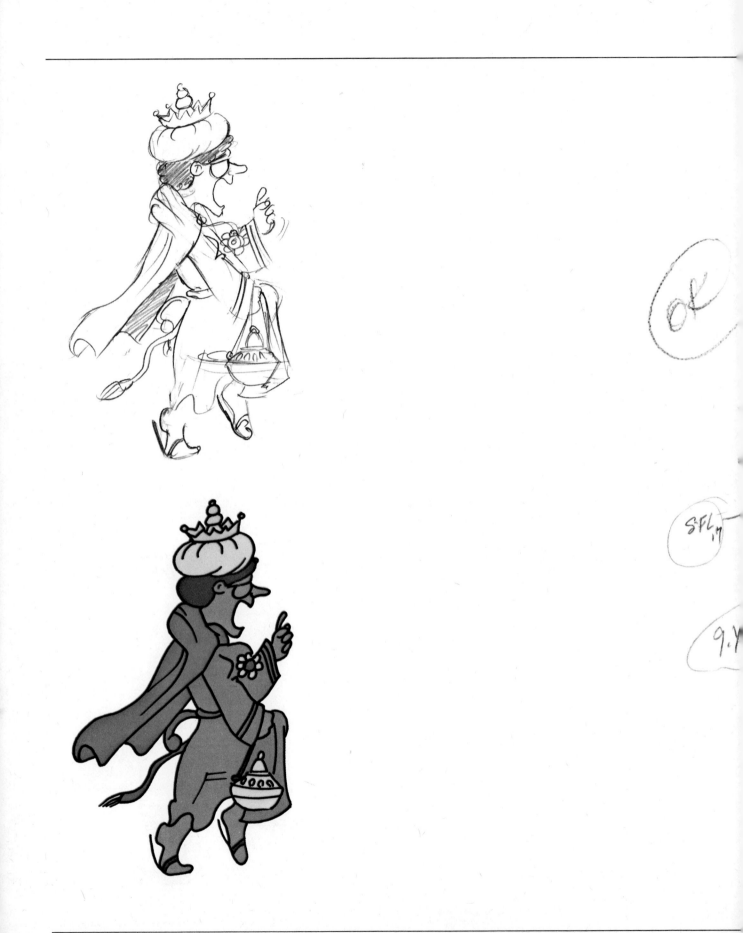

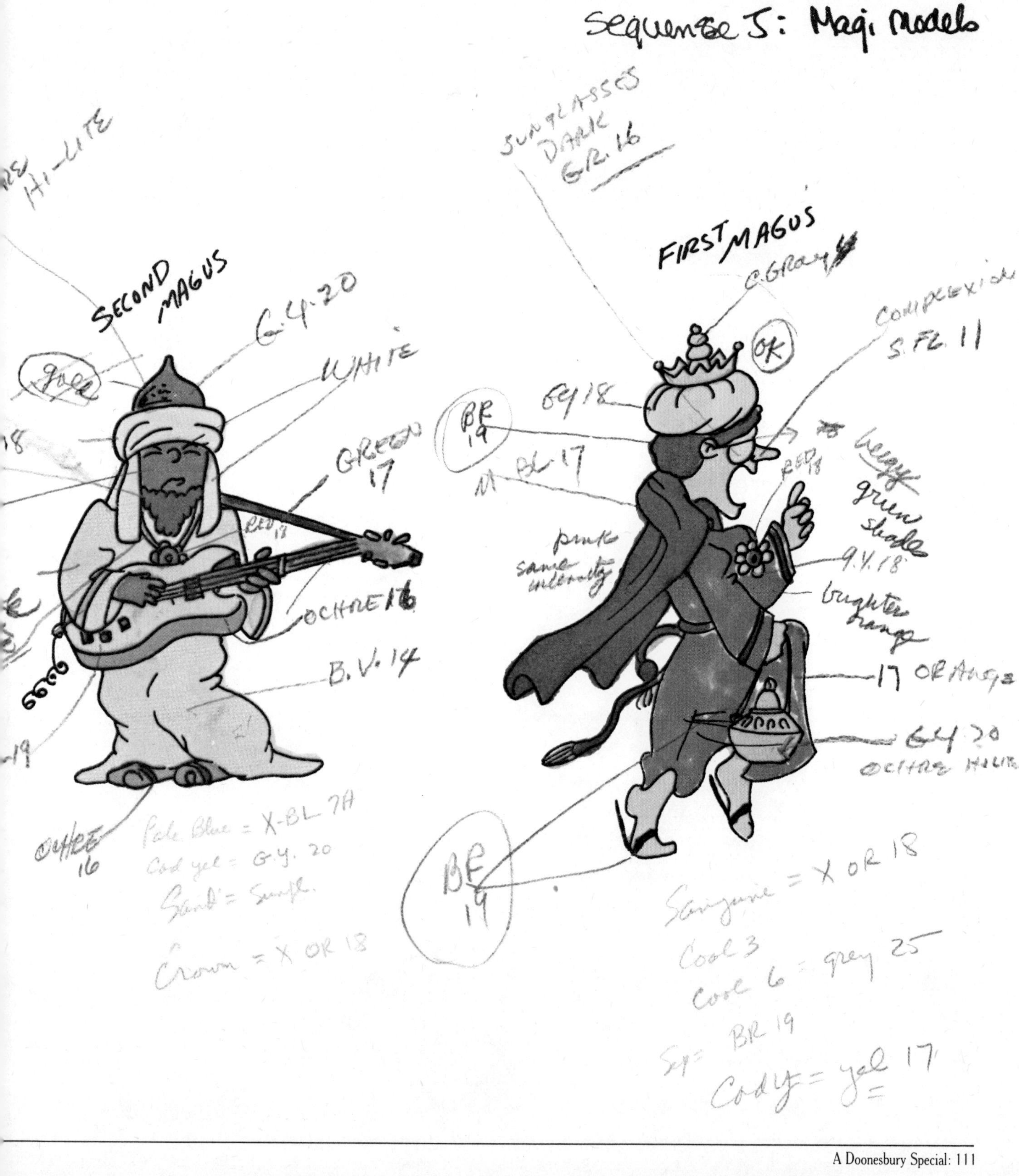
Sequence J: Magi models
SUNGLASSES DARK GR. 16
FIRST MAGUS
C. GRAY
COMPLEXION S. FL. 11
OK
GY 18
BR 19
M BL 17
RED 18
pink same intensity
green shade
G.Y. 18
brighter orange
17 ORANGE
GY 20 OCHRE HILITE
BR 19
SECOND MAGUS
HI-LITE
G.Y. 20
WHITE
GREEN 17
RED 18
OCHRE 16
B.V. 14
OCHRE 16
Pale Blue = X-BL 7A
Cool yel = G.Y. 20
Crown = X OR 18
Sanguine = X OR 18
Cool 3
Cool 6 = grey 25
BR 19
Cody = yel 17

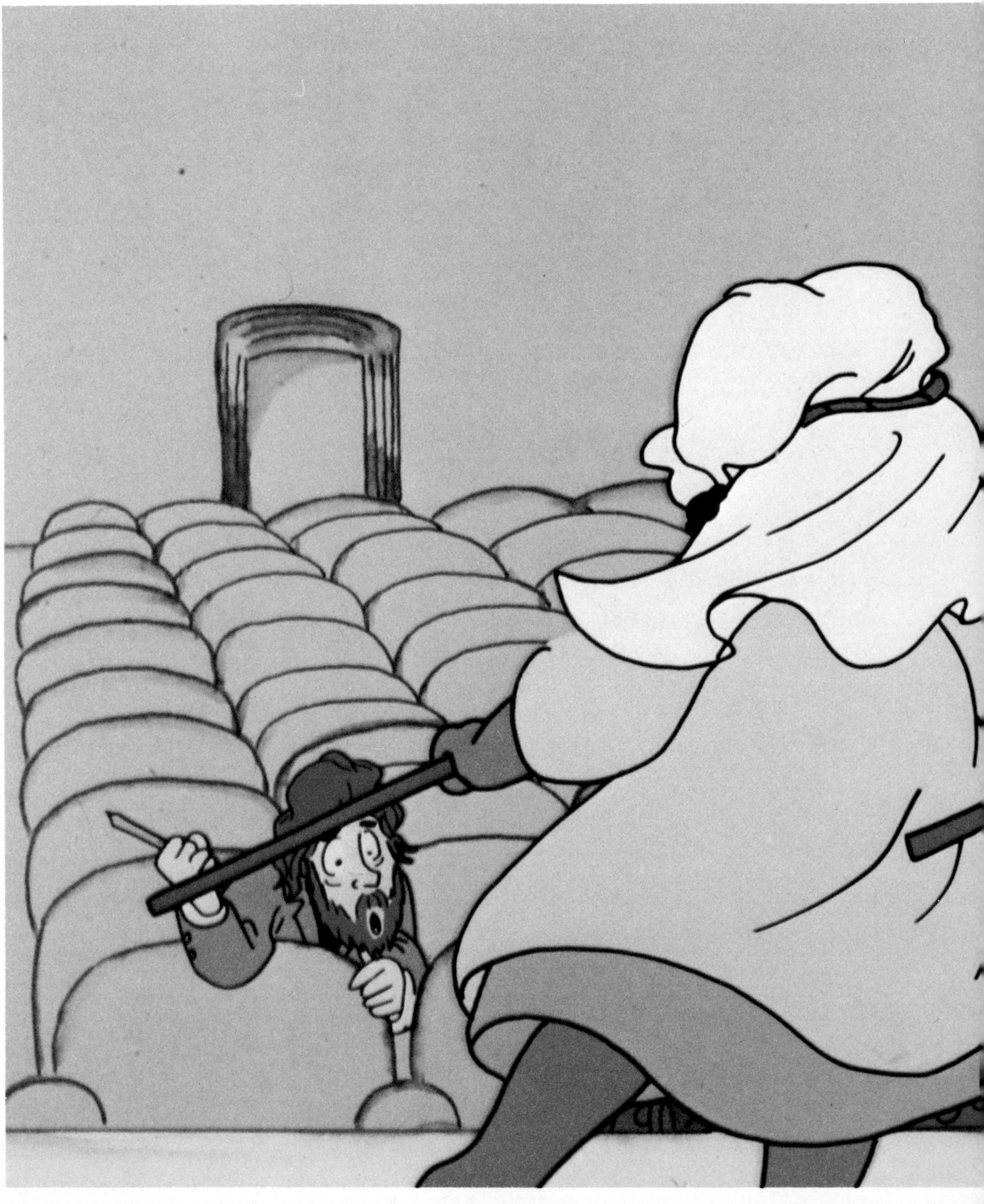

SCOT
Where's the second wise man?! That chord was his cue!

MAGUS
Off-stage
Sorry, Rev! I couldn't find my crown...

SCOT
C'mon, man, get it together! Joseph, take it from the top again! Let's get it right!

RUFUS
Verily, Mary, and here cometh another!

MAGUS
Bouncing on-stage
Myrrh is mine, a bitter perfume!
First magus, standing in background, starts playing atrocious guitar solo completely out of sync with song.

SCOT
Rushing up onto stage
No! No! No!
For the last time, the first magus does not lay down the rhythm guitar riff until after the flashback on the visitation!

RUFUS
To second magus
I thought the innkeeper was playing rhythm…

MAGUS
No, vibes.
Sound of audience beginning to arrive.

SCOT
Oh, no, people are arriving…all right, we'll just have to wing it!
Looks very ruffled
Places everyone! Jean, pull the curtain.
Curtain is closed on whole scene, except for lone mike and manger, which is lit from inside. Pause for backstage noises, guitar feedback. Scot finally steps out from behind the curtain, smooths down hair, smiles sheepishly. Light applause.

SCOT
Good evening and welcome to this year's Christmas Rock Pageant. In our show tonight, the parts are all played by the children of Walden Elementary School and the Walden Day-Care Center, with the exception of the part of Baby Jesus…
Gestures to manger with a smile
who is played by a hidden forty-watt light bulb.
Light bulb makes fizzing sound and goes out. Blackout.

RUFUS (Joseph)
aka

Mary is slightly taller than Joseph.

MARY

profile

The darkness is finally broken by a shaft of light, as Zonker opens the door of his closet. He is back at the commune, hanging up his dinner jacket. He changes quickly into his swimming suit and, grabbing his flippers, heads downstairs, passing Joanie and Mike in the kitchen. The screen door slams as Zonker heads out to the pond for an early evening dip. Conversation overheard in the kitchen as Mike and Joanie finish drying the dishes.

MIKE
Hey, these glasses are spotted. What if a neighbor drops by for ice tea?

JOANIE
Laughs
As Zonker walks down porch steps, Ellie appears on the horizon. They do not see each other. Zonker peels off to the right, humming to himself. Ellie approaches house, walks up steps and over to the kitchen window. Spying Joanie drying dishes, she taps gently on the window.

ELLIE
Joanie! Joanie!

JOANIE
Oh, hi, Ellie!

ELLIE
Whatcha doing dishes for, Sister? We're going to be late for our women's group!

JOANIE
Hold on…almost through.
To Mike
Mike, go out and entertain the wave of the future, will you?

MIKE
Walks toward door, shaking head and smiling
Women's group?
Walks through door out onto porch
Hi, Ellie.

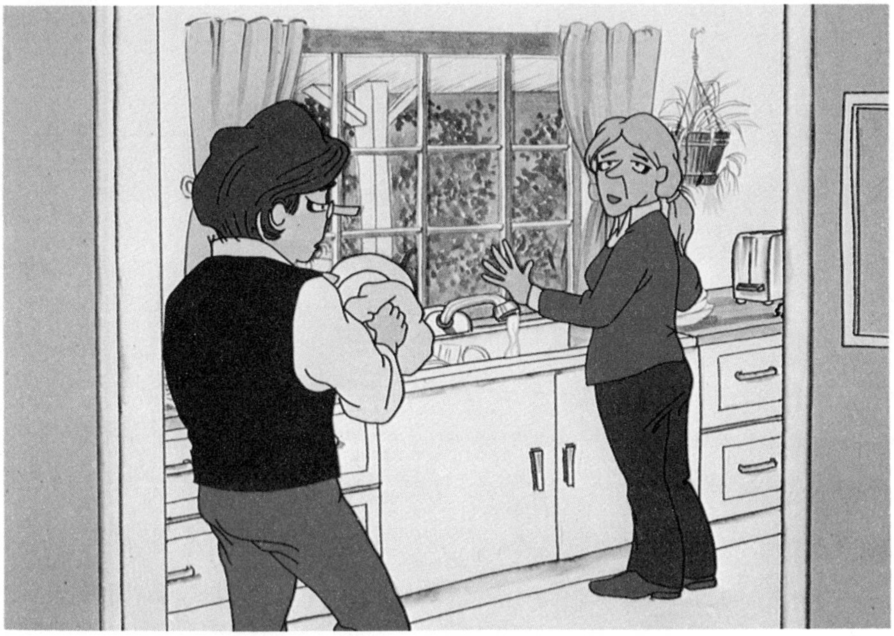

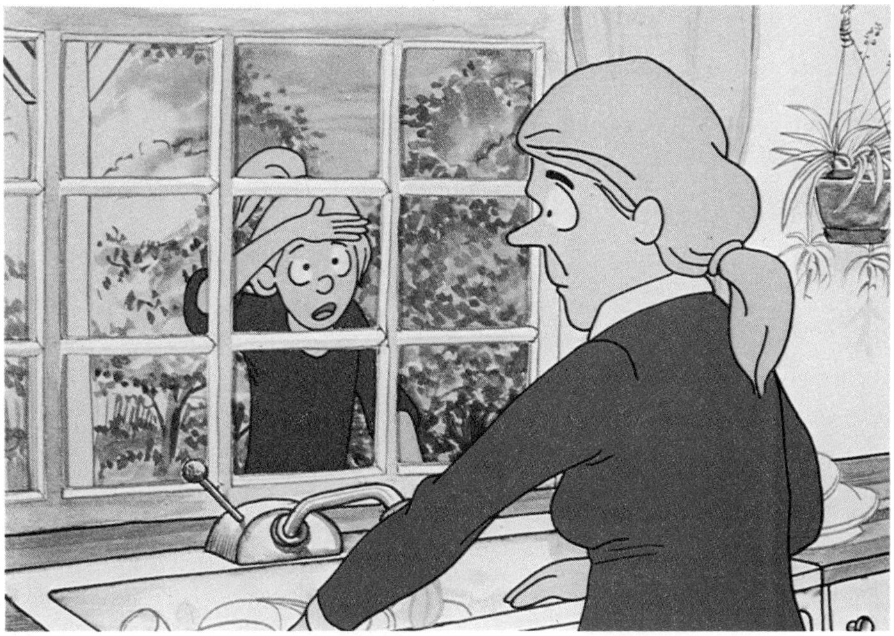

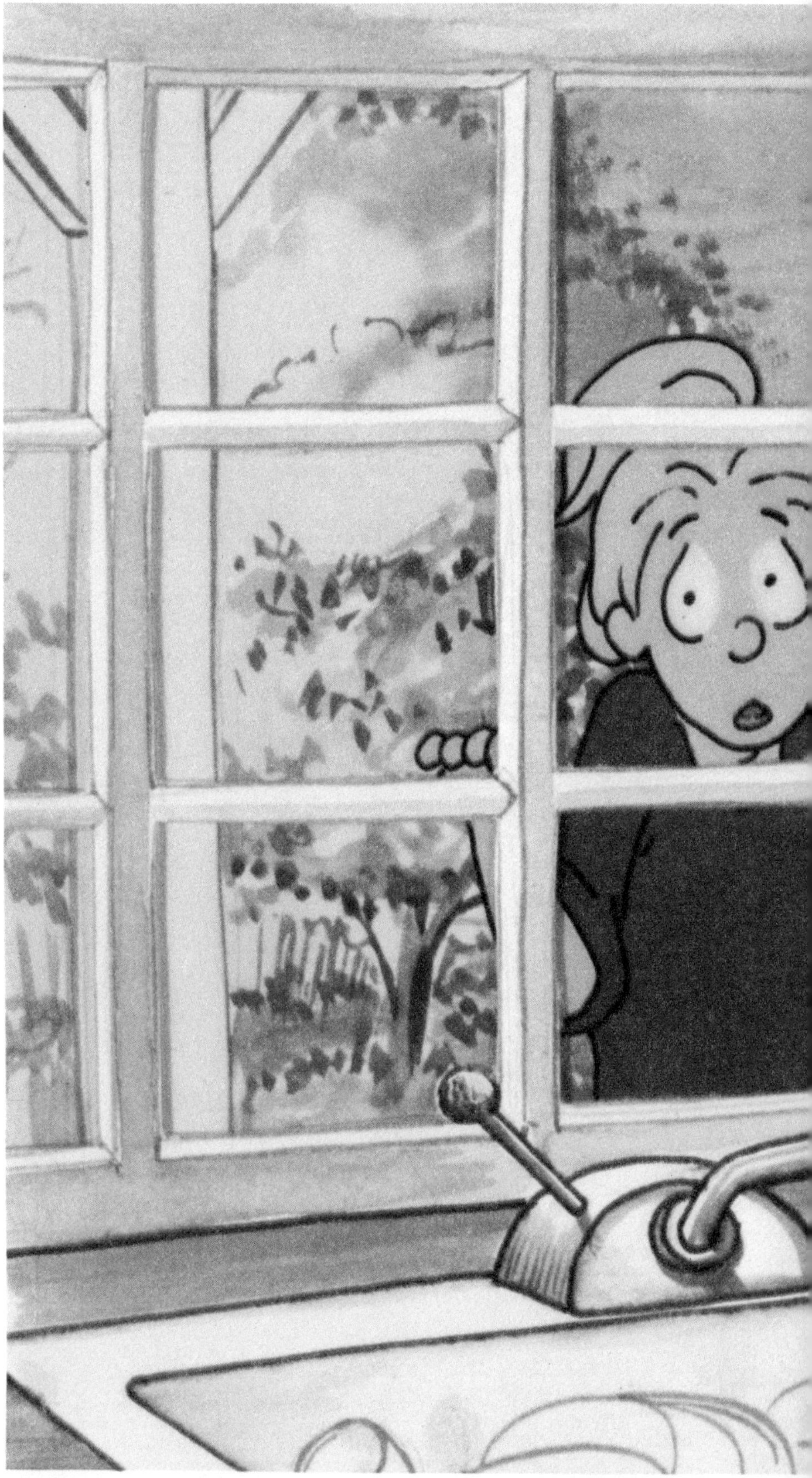

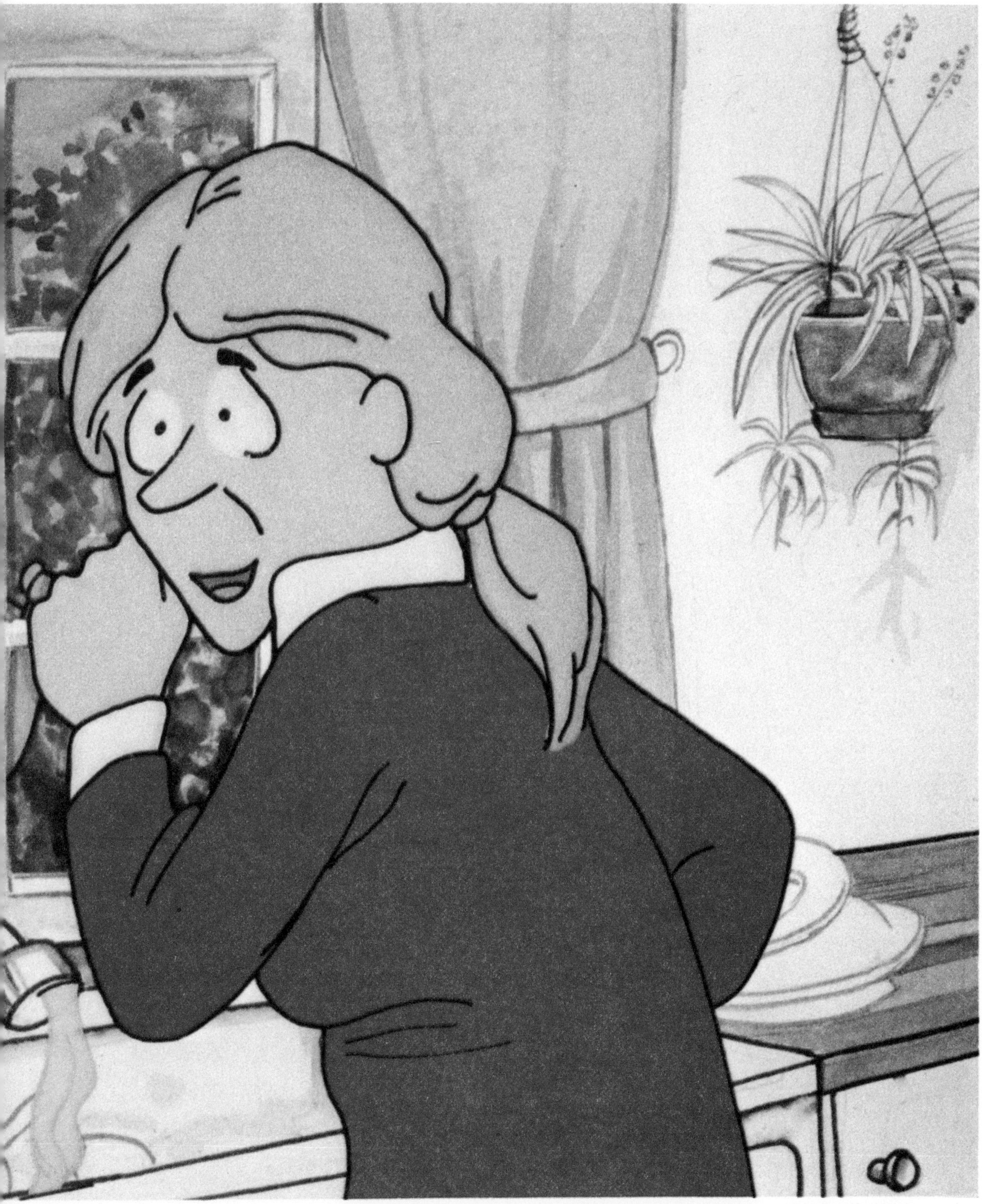

ELLIE
Pointing to Joanie through window
How come you got her doing the dishes, Mike?

MIKE
Sternly
It's her turn, Ellie.
Sits down on porch steps
She'll be out in a minute.

ELLIE
Oh…sorry…
Walks over to Mike and sits down next to him
I didn't mean to be strident or anything.

MIKE
Smiling
That's okay.
Pause
I been there.

ELLIE
You? Aw, c'mon…When? During the Revolution?

MIKE
Smiles, looks at her
The Revolution? What could you know about the Revolution?

ELLIE
Lots of stuff…it was against…um…what's his name, Nixon…and it was…um…fun, and usually held outdoors.

MIKE
Well, it was a little more complicated than that…it was a lot more complicated than that…
Sighs and looks out at sunset
As a matter of fact, we're still all trying to figure it out…

ELLIE
Even as we speak?

MIKE
Even as we speak…

ELLIE
Well, what happened to everyone after it was over? Do you keep in touch? Do you have a newsletter or something?

MIKE
Um…no…we…
Hear screen door slam. Joanie walks across porch.

JOANIE
Okay, Slim, let's get goin'…

ELLIE
To Mike as she gets up
Well, I really think you should consider a newsletter.

JOANIE
Be back in a couple of hours, Mike.
Joanie takes Ellie's hand and starts to walk down path.

ELLIE
'Bye, Mike. Hope you figure out what happened to everyone.
Off-camera splash. Pan to puddle, from which snorkle is visible. Trees around puddle are just starting to turn.

ZONKER
What happened to everyone? Oh, nothin' special. Just caring in different ways. Feeling the present as it moves by. Things gotta change, right?
Rustling leaves above turn a little more gold. A few fall onto the surface of the pond.
And the trees agree.
Pause
Good goin', trees.
Pull back as sun sets on horizon.

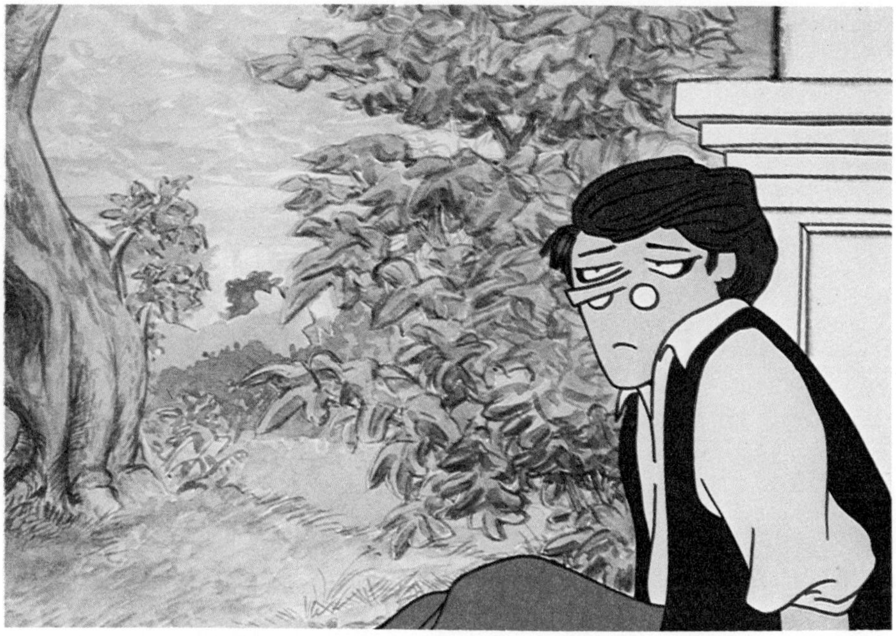

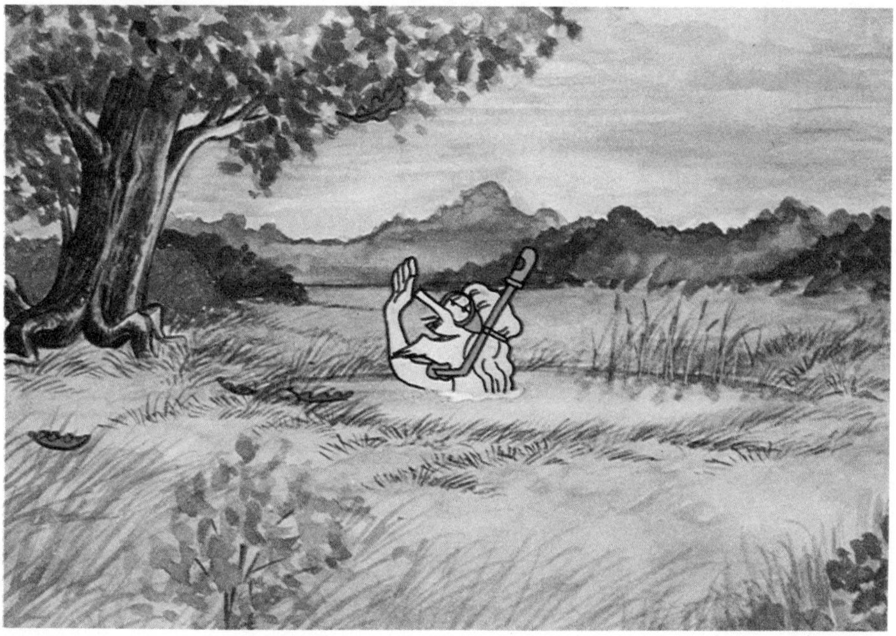

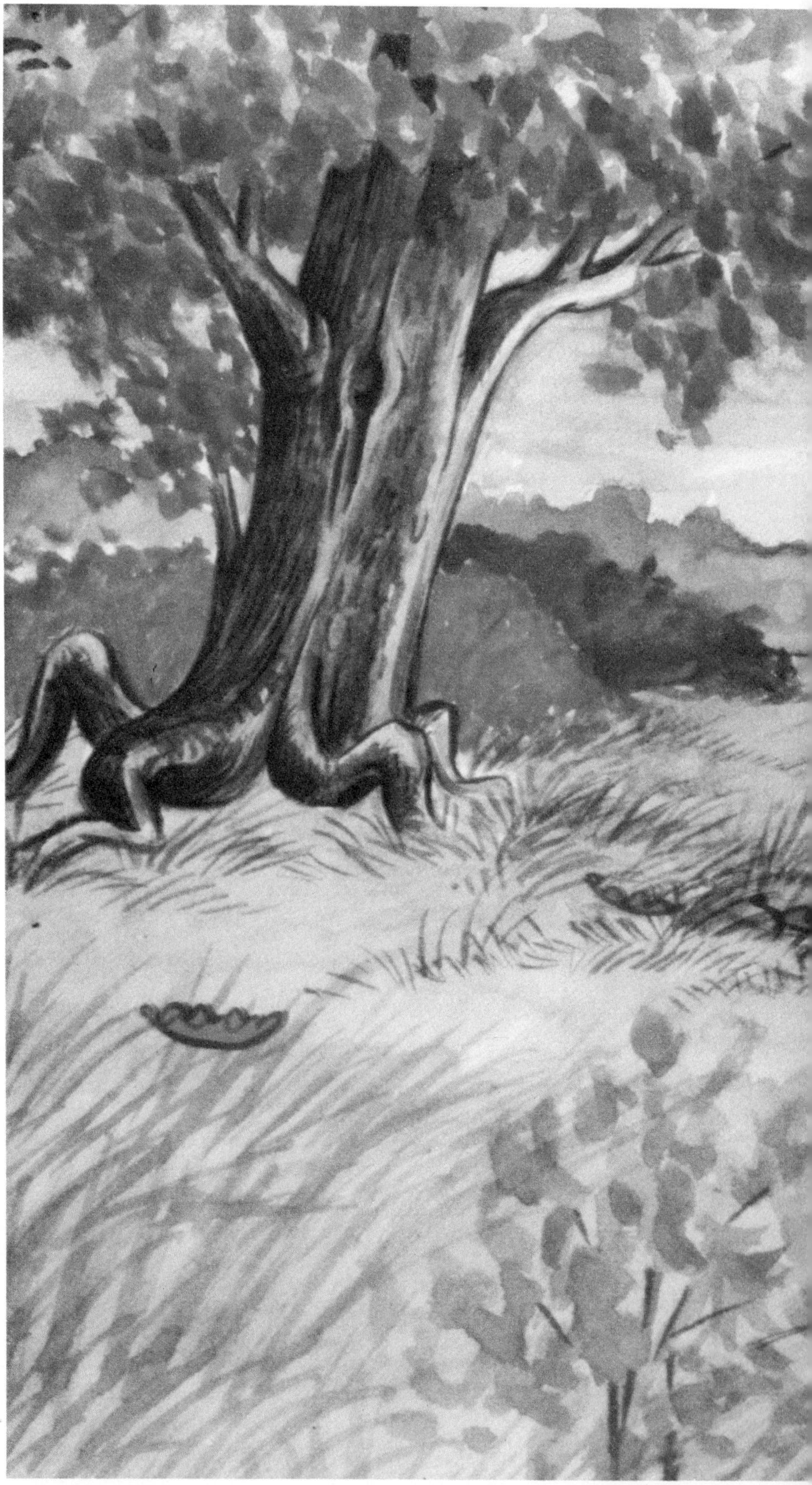

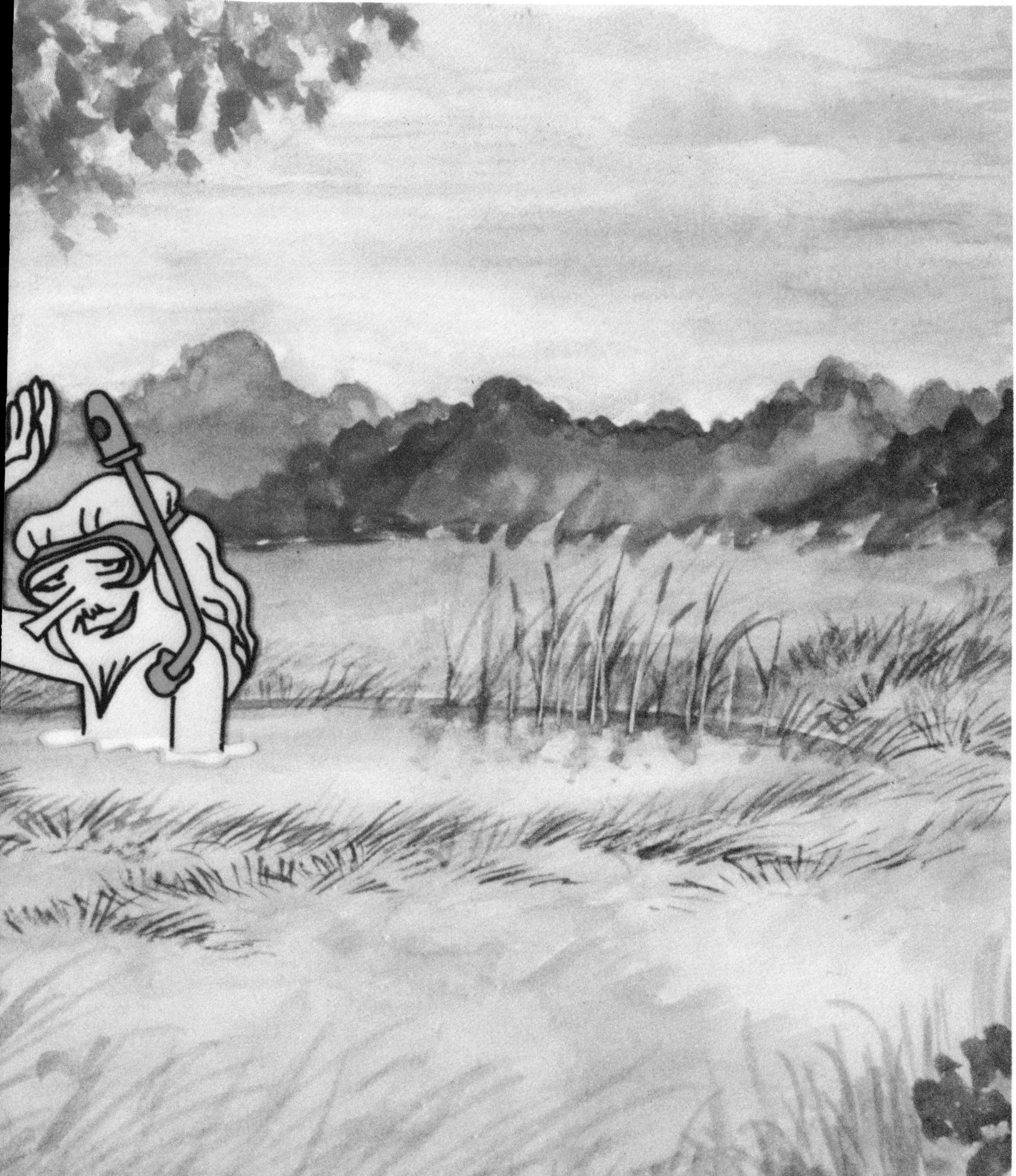

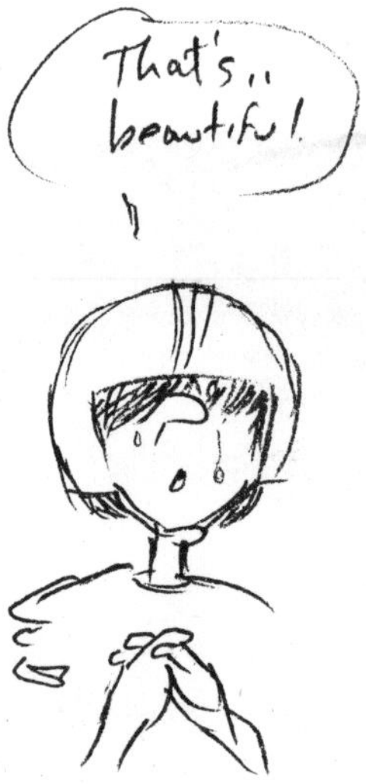
That's..
beautiful.